The Big Ideas Club Presents

Poetic Philosophy

Narrative Translations Designed for Accessibility

Aristotle's De Anima (On the Soul)

Three Analogies of Wax

By Aristotle

Translated by Jason Kassel, PhD

Introduction

Reading De Anima with philosophical seriousness means asking: what does it mean for life itself to have structure? This translation responds to that question by crafting a conceptual lexicon designed not to simplify Aristotle's thinking, but to preserve the precise tensions that animate it.

Aristotle's De Anima unfolds like a conceptual drama - one whose protagonist is the Life-Principle (ψυχή, psychē): that which gives Being to a living being.

The structure of the work follows a metaphysical ascent. It begins by questioning what kind of thing this Life-Principle might be (Book I), explores how it is bound to a Natural-Life Body (Book II), and concludes by tracing how this unified being Apprehends, Thinks, Desires, and Moves (Book III). Each stage expands and refines the previous one, in a spiraling movement from essence to operation, from cause to actualized motion.

Book I: Surveying What Has Been Said

1: Situating the "What-is-It?" Methodologically

Among things Noble (καλῶν, kalōn) and worthy of Honor (τιμίων, timiōn), we suppose Apprehension-of-Form (εἴδησις, eidēsis) to be superior to another either on the basis of its Precision (κατ᾽ ἀκρίβειαν, kat' akribeian), or because the things it concerns are both Better (βελτιόνων, beltionōn) and more Wondrous (θαυμασιωτέρων, thaumasiōterōn). For both of these reasons, it is reasonable to place the Inquiry (ζήτησις, zētēsis) into the Life-Principle (ψυχή, psychē) among the First-Things (πρῶτα, prōta). And, indeed, Knowledge (ἐπιστήμη, epistēmē) of it seems to contribute greatly toward the whole of Truth (ἀλήθεια, alētheia), and especially toward Understanding (γνῶσις, gnōsis) Nature (φύσις, physis). For the Life-Principle is an Origin-Principle (ἀρχή, archē) of all Living-Beings (ζῷα, zōia).

We seek to Observe (θεωρεῖν, theōrein) and to come to Know (γνῶναι, gnōnai) both the Nature and the Essence (οὐσία, ousia) of the Life-Principle, as well as everything that has Arisen-in-Relation-to (συμβέβηκε, symbebēke). Some of these seem to be Attributes (ἴδια πάθη, idia pathē) that belong solely to the Life-Principle; others seem to exist (ὑπάρχειν, hyparchein) through it in the Living-Beings themselves. Yet in every way, and by all Accounts (λόγοι, logoi), the Life-Principle is one of the most difficult things to gain any trustworthy Understanding of.

For the Question (ζήτημα, zētēma) at hand is one shared by many other Inquiries - namely the question concerning Essence: "What-is-It?" (τὸ τί ἐστι, to ti esti) And perhaps someone might think that there is a single Method (μέθοδος, methodos) common to all such Inquiries, as if the Account of things said to belong "by accident" followed one Method for all Case-in-Circumstance (περιπτώσεις, periptōseis). If that were so, then this is the Method we must seek out. But if there is not one single and common Method for grasping "What-is-It?", then the Task (πραγμάτευσις, pragmateusis) becomes still more difficult - for it will be necessary to determine what kind of Approach (ὁδός, hodos) applies for each Case-in-Particular (καθ᾽ ἕκαστον, kath' hekaston). And even if it becomes clear, should it be a Demonstration (ἀπόδειξις, apodeixis) or a Division (διαίρεσις, diairesis)? Or some other Method altogether?

There still remain many Puzzles (ἀπορίαι, aporiai) and Mis-Directions (πλάναι, planai) - about with what we are to Begin (ἄρξασθαι, arxasthai). For different things Begin from different Starting-Points (ἀρχαί, archai), just as in numbers and surfaces .So first, perhaps, it is necessary to distinguish to which Genus (γένος, genos) the Life-Principle belongs, and what kind of Being (ὄν, on) it is. Whether it is a This-Something (τόδε τι, tode ti), and a kind of Essence - or, rather, a Quality (ποιόν, poion), a Quantity (ποσόν, poson), or some of the other Categories (κατηγορίαι, katēgoriai) already laid out. We must also ask whether it exists in Potentiality (δύναμις, dynamis) or rather in Actualized-Unity (ἐντελέχεια, entelecheia) - for that makes a great difference. And we must consider as well whether it is Divisible (μεριστή, meristē) or Not-Divisible (ἀμερής, amerēs), and whether the whole Life-Principle is of a single Form (εἶδος, eidos), or not. And if not, whether the differences arise by Form or by Genus. As things stand now, those who speak and Inquire about the Life-Principle seem to be Examining (ἐπισκοπεῖν, episkopein) only the Human One (ἡ κατ᾽ ἄνθρωπον, hē kat' anthrōpon).

But one must be careful to notice whether the Account we give of it is of the Universal Life-Principle (ψυχὴ καθόλου, psychē katholou), as one would speak of "Animal" in general - or rather of each kind separately: the Life-Principle of a horse, or of a dog, or of a human, or of a god. For the universal "Animal" is not something that exists (ὑπάρχει, hyparchei) apart from the Individual (ἕκαστα ζῷα, hekasta zōia) animals, and the same goes for any other general Category that might be predicated in common. Moreover, if there are not many Life-Principles, but only Parts (μέρη, merē) of one, we must ask whether it is right to investigate the Whole Life-Principle first, or rather the Parts. Yet even this is difficult to determine -

which Parts differ from others Naturally (φύσει, physei), and whether we should first Examine the Parts themselves or the Functions (ἔργα, erga) they carry out, such as Sense-Apprehension (αἴσθησις, aisthēsis) or Thinking (νοεῖν, noein), or, rather, the Capacities (δυνάμεις, dynameis) to Apprehend-Sense (αἰσθάνεσθαι, aisthanesthai) and to Think (νοεῖν, noein). And the same question arises with the others. If the Functions come first, then someone might ask whether the Object-of-Apprehension (ἀντικείμενον, antikeimenon) - namely, the Sense-Apprehendable (αἰσθητόν, aisthēton) - should be Examined before the Individual Sense-Apprehender (αἰσθητικόν, aisthētikon)? Or, do we place the Intelligible-Object (νοητόν, noēton) before the Intellectual-Subject (νοητικόν, noētikon)?

It seems that coming to Know "What-is-It?" is not only useful for seeing the Causes (αἰτίαι, aitiai) of things that happen to belong to a given Essence - as, for example, in Mathematics (τὰ μαθηματικά, ta mathēmatika), knowing what Straightness (εὐθύ, euthy) and Curvature (καμπύλον, kampylon) are, or what a Line (γραμμή, grammē) and a Plane (ἐπίπεδον, epipedon) are, helps us grasp how many right-angles are in a triangle - but also, in turn, the Accidental-Features (συμβεβηκότα, symbebēkota) help us know the "What-is-It?" more fully. For when we are able to account for Appearances (φαινόμενα, phainomena) in terms of what happens by Accident (κατὰ συμβεβηκός, kata symbebēkos) - whether in all Cases or most of them - then we are best equipped to speak about Essence itself. For every Act (πρᾶξις, praxis) of Demonstration (ἀπόδειξις, apodeixis) begins from the "What-is-It?". And so, for any Definition (ὁρισμός, horismos) whose Accidental-Features fail to arise - or even fail to offer a plausible likeness - it is clear that the Definition is merely Dialectical (διαλεκτικός, dialektikos) and Empty (κενός, kenos).

2: Motion, Dust Motes, Floating Numbers, Elements

　　To begin the Inquiry into the Life-Principle, we must simultaneously Examine what must be clarified and, moving forward, take along the views of earlier thinkers - any who have ever made pronouncements about it - so that we may adopt what has been Rightly-

Said (εὖ εἰρημένον, eu eirēmenon) and guard ourselves against what has been Poorly-Said (κακῶς εἰρημένον, kakōs eirēmenon). We must begin with what most clearly appears to belong to the Life-Principle by Nature.

The Ensouled-Body (ἔμψυχον, empsychon) is said to differ from the Not-Ensouled-Body (ἄψυχον, apsychon) most of all in two ways: in Motion (κίνησις, kinēsis) and in Sense-Apprehension (αἴσθησις, aisthēsis). And from the Ancients, we have inherited almost exactly these two Attributes (συμβεβηκότα, symbebēkota) in their Accounts of the Life-Principle. Some of them, especially the earliest, declare that the Life-Principle is precisely that which causes Motion. Since they believed that nothing that is Not-Moved (ἀκίνητον, akinēton) can itself Move (κινέω, kineō) anything else, they assumed that the Life-Principle must be one of the Moving (κινοῦν, kinoun) things. This is why Democritus claimed that the Life-Principle is a kind of Fire or Heat. Among the Infinite (ἄπειρα, apeira) Shapes (σχήματα, schēmata) and Not-Divisible Elements (ἄτομα, atoma), he identified the

Spherical (σφαιροειδῆ, sphairoeidē) ones with Fire and the Life-Principle - like the so-called dust motes seen floating in sunlight, the swirls visible in rays that pass through window slits - which he called the Seed-Elements (ἀρχαί, archai) of all Nature. Leucippus agreed.

These Spherical-Atoms, he said, form the Life-Principle because they are the most able to pass through everything with ease, Moving themselves and Moving other things. They concluded that the Life-Principle is that which imparts Motion to Living-Beings. And for that Reason (λόγος, logos), they claimed that the Act-of-Breathing (ἀναπνοή, anapnoē) is the criterion for Being-Alive - since the surrounding Medium (τὸ περιέχον, to periechon) compresses Living-Bodies (τὰ ἔμψυχα σώματα, ta empsycha sōmata) and squeezes out the particles responsible for Motion, the Living-Body needs support from outside, through Inhalation (εἴσπνοια, eispnoia) because the Spherical-Elements themselves never rest. By drawing in new ones, the Organism (ζῷον, zōion) prevents its Inner-Elements (τὰ ἔνδοθεν, ta endothen) from escaping under the Medium's pressure, restraining what is being compacted and giving structure. As long as it can do this, a Being Lives (ζῇ, zēi).

This idea resembles what some of the speakers in the market-place (ἀγορᾶν, agoran) have said: that the same Intelligence (διάνοια, dianoia) belongs to all such Beings. Some claimed that the Life-Principle is the Spherical motes floating in Air (ἀήρ, aēr); others said it is whatever Moves those Spherical motes. They speak this way because the motes are always seen in Motion, even when the air is completely still. All of these views share the same direction: that the Life-Principle is That-Which-Moves (τὸ κινοῦν, to kinoun). These thinkers seem to have assumed that Motion is the most proper and intimate Characteristic of the Life-Principle, that everything else is Moved because of it - while it is Moved by itself. For nothing can be seen to cause Motion unless it also is in Motion.

Likewise, Anaxagoras declared that the Life-Principle is the Mover (κινοῦν, kinoun). And anyone else who said that Mind (νοῦς, nous) Moved the All (τὸ πᾶν, to pan) would align with this - though not in the same way as Democritus. Democritus simply identified Life-Principle and Mind as "One and the-Same" (ταὐτόν, tauton): What-Appears (δοκοῦν, dokoun) is What-is-True (ἀληθές, alēthes). He even praised Homer for saying, "Hector had lost his mind," as if to suggest that using Mind isn't about Grasping (λαμβάνειν, lambanein) Truth by Capacity but is merely Being-Animated (ψυχοῦσθαι, psychousthai). For him, the Life-Principle and Mind are Not-Distinct.

Anaxagoras was less clear. In some places, he says that Mind is the Cause of what is Well-Formed (εὐσχημόνως, euschēmonōs) and Right (ὀρθῶς, orthōs); elsewhere, he identifies Mind with the Life-Principle itself. He says it is present in all Living-Things, great and small, noble and base. Yet the kind of Mind spoken of as Thoughtful (φρόνιμος, phronimos) does not appear to exist equally in all animals - or even in all humans. So then, those who looked toward Motion in the Ensouled-Body supposed that the Life-Principle was what was most Mobile (κινητικώτατον, kinētikōtaton). Others, who focused on Knowing and Apprehending what exists, said the Life-Principle is the Origin-Points (ἀρχαί, archai) of these Capacities - some proposing many such Origins, some only one.

For instance, Empedocles said the Life-Principle is made of all the Elements (στοιχεῖα, stoicheia), and that each is a Life-Principle in itself. He wrote:

"We have seen Earth (γῆ, gē) by means of Earth,

Water (ὕδωρ, hydōr) by means of Water,

Divine Aether (αἰθήρ, aithēr) by Aether,

and Fire by Fire-Unseen (πῦρ ἀφανές, pyr aphanes).

Love (φιλότης, philotēs) by Love,

and Strife (νεῖκος, neikos) by Hateful Strife."

In a similar fashion, Plato, in the Timaeus, constructed the Life-Principle from the Elements, since Like (ὅμοιον, homoion) is Known by Like, and things are made from their Elemental-Principles (στοιχειῶν ἀρχῶν, stoicheiōn archōn). Likewise, in the writings attributed to the Philosophers, it was defined that the Living-Creature (ζῷον, zōion) itself derives from the "Idea of the-One" (ἰδέα τοῦ ἑνός, idea tou henos) and the First-Dimensions (πρῶτα σχήματα, prōta schēmata) - length, breadth, and depth - and the rest follow in a similar pattern. Further still, some have drawn distinctions this way: they assigned the One to Mind, but Two to

Knowledge - since the former pertains only to Unity, while the Number (ἀριθμός, arithmos) of the Plane was aligned with Opinion, and the Number of the Solid with Apprehension. For they claimed Numbers were both the Form-Apprehensions themselves and the Originating-Principles (ἀρχαί, archai) - and that these Numbers came from the Elements. Things, they said, are discerned either by Mind, by Knowledge, by Opinion, or by Apprehension; and the kinds of Numbers they spoke of were the Form-Apprehensions corresponding to each of these.

Since the Life-Principle was believed to be both a source of Motion and a Knower, some thinkers wove together these traits, asserting that the Life-Principle is a Self-Moving Number (ἀριθμὸς αὐτοκίνητος, arithmos autokinētos), formed from both Capacities. But they differ about the Principles - what they are and how many. Most especially this occurs among those who define things in terms of Bodies, as opposed to those who claim Principles exist in both Body and Number. They also disagree on the Quantity: some say there is one Principle, others that there are many. According to each of these views, they accordingly assign different Attributes to the Life-Principle.

Those who take Motion to be Most-Essential (κυριώτατον, kuriōtaton) among the Primary-Things (πρῶτα, prōta) do not Reason poorly in making this so.

That is why some have claimed the Life-Principle is Fire - since Fire is the most subtle and least Corporeal of the Elements, and also the one that Moves and causes Movement most fundamentally. Democritus went further, giving more precision to his account. He identified Life-Principle and Mind as the same thing - and he described this as composed of the finest and most Indivisible Bodies, attributing its Capacity to Move to their minuteness and shape. Among all shapes, he said, the Spherical is most mobile, and both Fire and Mind are of this sort.

Anaxagoras, as mentioned before, seems to distinguish between Life-Principle and Mind, though he also treats them as if they share a single Nature. Yet he especially elevates Mind as the First-Principle (πρώτη ἀρχή, prōtē archē) of All (τὸ πᾶν, to pan), saying that it alone among Beings is Simple, Unmixed, and Pure (ἁπλοῦν καὶ ἀμιγὲς καὶ καθαρόν, haploun kai amiges kai katharon). He assigns to Mind both the Capacity of Knowing and the Capacity of Motion, stating that it is Mind which Moved the All.

Thales too - based on what is remembered of him - appears to have thought the Life-Principle something that Moves, for he said that a magnet has a Life-Principle because it causes iron to Move.

Diogenes, like others, supposed Air (ἀήρ, aēr) to be the subtlest of all things and the First-Principle. Thus, he claimed the Life-Principle both Knows and Moves because Air, as the most refined substance, is capable of causing both Apprehension and Motion.

Heraclitus likewise claimed that the Origin was the Life-Principle, provided that one takes the Rising-Vapor (ἀτμίς, atmis) to be the Source (ἀρχή, archē) of everything else. This he considered the most incorporeal and the most perpetually in Flux (ῥεῦμα, rheuma). And he thought that what Moves is Known only by what is also Moving. All-Things (πάντα, panta), he claimed, are in Motion - and many others agreed.

Alcmaeon seems to have thought similarly regarding the Life-Principle. He said it was Immortal (ἀθάνατον, athanaton), because it resembles the Immortals - meaning that it is always in Motion. For Divine-Things (θεῖα, theia) too are said to be in continual and ceaseless motion: the Moon, the Sun, the Stars, and the entire Heavens.

Some of the more heavy-handed thinkers declared even Water (ὕδωρ, hydōr) to be the Life-Principle, like Hippo. They seem to have been persuaded by the role of Moisture (ὑγρόν, hygron) in Reproduction, since all Generation begins from the Moist. Those who claimed Blood (αἷμα, haima) to be the Life-Principle did so because the generative fluid is not itself blood - but they called it the Primary-Form (πρῶτον εἶδος, prōton eidos) of Life-Principle. Others, like Critias, directly named Blood as the Life-Principle, assuming that Sense-Apprehension is most intimately bound up with the Life-Principle, and that Blood, by its Nature, is what enables it.

3: Two Senses of Motion (and Digression into Mind)

We must begin by examining the question of Motion. For, it may not only be Not-True (οὐκ ἀληθές, ouk alēthes) - as some assert - that the Essence of the Life-Principle is to Move Itself or to have the Capacity to Move; it may also be entirely Not-Possible (ἀδύνατον, adynaton) for Motion to belong to the Life-Principle in this way. Already, it has been said that what causes Motion is not always itself in Motion. Every Mover exists in two modes: either in itself or in another. When something is called a Mover by being in another, its Motive power arises only insofar as it is inside something else that is moving - like a passenger aboard a ship. For it is the ship that truly Moves, while the passenger Moves only accidentally, by being carried along with it. This distinction becomes clear when we consider bodily limbs. The proper Motion of the foot is walking, and this is a Motion that belongs also to the Whole human. But such Motion does not belong to the passenger, whose Body Moves only by being inside the moving ship. So, since there are two senses in which something can be "in Motion," we must now Inquire whether the Life-Principle Moves Itself in its own right - from within, and by Nature.

Of the kinds of Motion (Movement by Place, by Quality, by Increase or Decrease, or by Coming-to-Be and Passing-Away) if the Life-Principle truly Moves, then it must partake in one or several of these. But if its Motion is by Nature, and not merely Accidental, then Motion must belong to its very Essence. And in that case, it must also possess Place - for all Motion unfolds in Place. Moreover, if the Being of the Life-Principle is to Move itself, then its Motion is not Accidental, like Whiteness or Length. Whiteness is only said to Move when its bearer - a Body - Moves. Thus, Whiteness has no Place in itself. But if Motion belongs by Nature to the Life-Principle, then it would necessarily possess a Natural Place. And further: if it Moves by Nature, then even when it Moves by force, the Motion would remain Natural. The same logic applies to rest: what the Life-Principle comes to rest in by Nature, it must also Move toward by Nature; and likewise for forced Motion and rest. Yet, it is difficult to say what kind of Motion or rest might belong to the Life-Principle by Force - difficult even for one who freely invents causes. If it Moves upward, it would seem to be of Fire; if downward, of Earth - for these are the Natural directions of those Elements. The same reasoning would apply for intermediate kinds of Body.

Now, since the Life-Principle appears to be what causes the Body to Move, it would be reasonable to think that it Moves in the same way that it causes the Body to Move. And so, we might also say the reverse: the Motion by which the Body is Moved is the Motion by which the Life-Principle Moves. But the Body is Moved by displacement - that is, Motion by Place. Therefore, the Life-Principle too must change Place - either as a Whole or in Part - when the Body does. And if so, then it would also be able to depart and return; and perhaps, this reentry could explain the revival of animals once thought dead. Yet even Accidental Motion may come from an External-Force, as when a Living-Thing is pushed. Still, it is Not-Suitable for something whose Nature is to Move Itself to be Moved by another - except by Accident. Just as something that is Good in itself or for its own sake cannot be said to exist for the sake of another, so too a Self-Mover must not be Moved by something else.

Perhaps someone will say that the Life-Principle is Moved especially by Perceptible things - if it is Moved at all. But even if it does Move Itself, it would still be the Mover - and therefore, if every Motion involves a kind of "ec-stasis" (ἔκστασις), a standing-out or displacement of what is Moved, then the Life-Principle would also be displaced from itself - unless its Motion is only accidental. Yet some assert that the Life-Principle's Motion is essential, occurring from within. Democritus, for example, offers a comic image - one also used by the playwright Philippus - saying that Daedalus caused a wooden statue of Aphrodite to Move by pouring quicksilver into it. Similarly, Democritus claimed that the Not-Divisible Spheres, because of their very Nature never to remain still, Move constantly, and by dragging the Body with them, they bring about the whole creature's Motion. But then, we must ask whether these same things could also produce Rest. And how they could do so is hard to say - or even impossible. On the whole, the Life-Principle does not seem to Move the Living-Being in this way. Rather, it Moves by a kind of Choice and Thought-Activity, as the Timaeus suggests: the Life-Principle Moves the Body because it Moves itself - since it is interwoven with the Body. Crafted from the Elements and apportioned according to Harmonic Number, the Life-Principle was made with a kind of Harmony - and with the Capacity of Sense-Apprehension suitable to Motion. The whole was bent into a Circular-Form so that its Motions would be consonant. From the One, two Circles were made and bound together. From one of these, a further Seven were divided - said to be both the Motions of the Heavens and of the Life-Principle. This all may be Beautifully-Said.

But to claim that the Life-Principle is a Magnitude is a mistake. Clearly, this model represents the Mind (νοῦς, nous) of the Cosmos - but that Mind is Not the same as the Sense-Apprehending Capacity of the Life-Principle, nor as the Desiring Capacity - whose Motions do not follow Circular-Patterns. Mind is One and Continuous - like Thought-Activity. And Thought-Activity proceeds through Objects of Thought (νοητά, noēta). These unfold in sequence, like Number - but Not like Spatial Magnitude. So Mind is Not-Continuous in the way a Body is; it is Not-Divisible, not by Parts, but by a different kind of Unity. For how could a Magnitude even Think? Would it Think with a Part? But if so, the Part is either a Point or a Portion. If it's a Point, and Points are infinite, then it would never finish Thinking. If it's a Portion, then it must Think the same thing over and over - either a finite or infinite number of times. But we observe that Understanding often occurs all at once. And if it is enough for Mind to make contact with just a Part of the

Object, why require Motion - especially Circular Motion - or even Magnitude at all? And if it must contact the whole Circle in order to think, what role does the contact of the Parts play? How could what is divisible Grasp what is indivisible? Or how could the indivisible be Apprehended by something divisible? We are told that Mind is this Circle because the Motion of Mind is Thought-Activity, and Circular Motion is Revolution. So if Thinking is Revolution, then Mind is a Circle, and its Revolution is the Mode of Thinking. But then it would always be Thinking - because Circular-Motion is Eternal. Yet Practical Thinking has an End, since it is always for the sake of something else. And Theoretical Thinking, too, is bounded by Argument: and every Argument is either a Definition or a Demonstration. Demonstrations begin from a First Principle and proceed toward a Conclusion -

they End, either with the Logical-Middle (μέσον, meson) or with the Result. If they do not reach an End, they do not Return-Again to the Beginning - but go Forward, adding new Middles and Ends. Circular-Motion, by contrast, returns again to the Origin-Start (ἀρχή, archē).

All Definitions are finite. So if the revolution is the same again and again, then Mind must Think the same thing again and again. Yet Thinking appears more like a kind of Rest than Motion - just as Reasoning seems more stable than mobile. And surely we would not call Thinking

Divine if it were difficult and strained. But if Motion is Not the Essence of the Life-Principle, then any Motion it has must be Not-Natural. This would be a grievous condition: for if the Life-Principle is mingled with the Body and cannot escape, that Mixture is something to flee - especially if it is better for Mind to be free from the Body, as many say and believe. Even the Cause of the Heavens' Circular-Motion is unclear. For it is Not the Essence of the Life-Principle that causes this Revolution - since it Moves this way only incidentally. Nor is it the Body. Rather, it is the Life-Principle that Moves the Body. And if one says that Circular-Motion is superior, that must be the reason why the god made the Life-Principle Move in a Circle: because it is better to be in Motion than at Rest, and better to Move in this way than in another. But this entire line of Inquiry belongs to another Discussion. Let us put it aside for now.

There is, however, something absurd that follows from all these Accounts - indeed, from most Accounts of the Life-Principle. For they affix it to the Body, place it within - but they do not say why or how, or what sort of Body it must be. Yet this ought to be essential - for whenever one thing Acts and another is Acted Upon, one Moves and the other is Moved, these relationships are Not random. Most thinkers speak only about what the Life-Principle is, but say nothing of the Body that receives it - as if any Life-Principle could enter any Body, like the Pythagorean tale of a wandering soul randomly taking up a Body by chance. But every Body appears to have its own specific Actualizing-Structure and Form (εἶδος, eidos). Their explanation would be like saying that carpentry enters flutes. But a Craft must have its Tools - just as the Life-Principle must have its Body.

4: Rejecting Harmony, Motion, and Numbers

Another Account has also been handed down concerning the Life-Principle, one that has persuaded many and seems no less plausible than the others already discussed. It claims its Reasoning as if presenting it for public review - aligning itself with familiar discourses. Some have declared that the Life-Principle is Harmony (ἁρμονία, harmonia). For Harmony, they say, is a Composition - a blending of Opposites - and the Body too is composed of Contraries. Yet, properly speaking, Harmony is either (1) a Proportional-Relation (λόγος) between the blended parts, or (2) the Product of a specific Composing-Process. But the Life-Principle cannot be either of these in any reasonable sense. Moreover, Motion (τὸ κινεῖν, to kinein) is not characteristic of Harmony - and yet everyone attributes the Capacity for Motion to the Life-Principle, more than to anything else. Harmony more properly describes Bodily Health, or generally the Bodily Virtue - Not something that belongs to the Life-

Principle. This becomes obvious when one tries to assign the Emotions or Actions of the Life-Principle to any kind of Harmony - for no such attribution can be made coherent. And if Harmony is understood to involve a joining of Parts - especially in things possessing Magnitude, Motion, and Position - then the Composing-Process would exclude the possibility of any further Affinity. It is from such exclusions that Accounts of Mixture arise. But these accounts are indecisive, and the Composition of the Body's Parts admits of many variations. So in what way - or from which Elements - could we reasonably suppose Mind (νοῦς, nous), or the

Capacity to Sense or to Desire, to be a Composition? It is equally absurd to claim that the Life-Principle is the Account of a Mixture. The Elemental-Mixture that composes Flesh is not the same as that which composes Bone. Would that mean that the Life-Principle changes depending on which Substance is involved? If so, there would be multiple Life-Principles in the same Body - since every bodily part arises from a different Mixture of Elements. And if the Account of the Mixture is Harmony, and Harmony is the Life-Principle, then each part would have its own separate Life-Principle. One could raise a similar challenge to Empedocles, who also asserts that each Element has its own distinct Proportional-Relation. Then we must ask: is that Ratio itself the Life-Principle?

Or is the Life-Principle something that arises within the Limbs from the Elements? And again: is Love (φιλία, philia) the cause of any and every Mixture? Or only of the well-composed, Ratio-Governed Mixtures? And in that case, is Love the Ratio itself, or is it something else entirely? These are the kinds of puzzles that such theories face. And if the Life-Principle is something other than the Mixture, why is it destroyed when the Flesh is destroyed - or when any other part of the Living-Being is ruined? And if Not every part has its own Life-Principle, yet the Life-Principle is still supposed to be the Ratio of the Mixture, then what is it that perishes when the Life-Principle departs? From all this, it becomes clear that the Life-Principle cannot be a Harmony - nor, for that matter, a Circle, as some claim.

Perhaps it is Moved Accidentally, as we discussed earlier, and perhaps it causes Motion in itself - like a thing that Moves inside the vessel that contains it. But this Motion would still come from the Life-Principle, and the Life-Principle itself would not strictly Move by spatial displacement. From this, some have supposed that the Life-Principle itself Moves - but that does not follow. For even if Sorrowing, Rejoicing, and Thinking are all species of Movement, and each may be called a Motion, the Motion arises through the Life-Principle - as when one becomes angry or afraid, and the Heart is stirred in a certain way. Perhaps Thinking too involves a kind of Internal-Motion - or else a completely different kind. (Some of these Motions arise by displacement, others by alteration. But a full treatment of their kinds and causes belongs to another Inquiry.) To say that the Life-Principle becomes Angry is like saying it builds or weaves. It is better to say: the Human-Being grows Angry or Learns or Thinks - through the Life-Principle. And Not in the sense that these Movements reside in the Life-Principle - but that sometimes they extend up to it, and sometimes they flow outward from it. Apprehension might come in from the Bodily-Organs toward the Life-Principle, while Memory might Move from the Life-Principle outward, toward stored Impressions or sensory deposits. Now, Mind (νοῦς, nous) seems to be something

that enters in as a kind of Essence - Not something that perishes. For if it could be destroyed, it would most of all be affected by old age. But perhaps old age does to Mind what it does to Sense-Apprehension: if an old man were to gain a youthful eye, he would see as well as the young. So aging is not due to some damage to the Life-Principle - but rather to the Body, just as occurs in drunkenness or illness. When Thinking or Contemplating becomes sluggish, it is due to some corruption in another Capacity - while the Mind itself remains unaffected. Thus, to Think, to Love, or to Hate - these are Not things that belong to Mind as such, but rather to the Composite-Being that possesses it - or, more precisely, to the Being in which it resides. So when that Composite-Unity is destroyed, these Actions too vanish - because they never belonged to Mind alone, but to the Shared-Whole. Mind itself may be something more Divine and Unaffected. From all this, it becomes clear that the Life-Principle does not Move on its own. And if it does not Move in general, then plainly it does not Move Itself.

The most Irrational View of all is the claim that the Life-Principle is a Number that Moves Itself. This leads to two impossibilities: first, from the Nature of Motion in general; and second, from the absurdity of treating Number in this way. For how could one imagine a Unit (μονάς, monas) to be Moved? By what? And how? It has no Parts, no distinctions. If a unit is both Mover and Moved, then it must differ from itself. And if, as they say, when a Point is Moved it becomes a Line, and a Line when Moved becomes a Plane - and that the Motion of Points yields Lines (since a Point is a Unit with Position) - then the Number assigned to the Life-Principle must already somehow include Position. But when a Unit or Number is removed from a larger Number, a different Number remains. Yet many plants and animals, when divided, still live - retaining the same kind of Life-Principle. So what difference does it make whether we call these Units or tiny Bodies? Even if one imagines that Democritus's Spheres break down into Points, and only Quantity remains, still there must be some distinction between What-Moves and What-is–Moved - just as in any continuous magnitude. The distinction lies not in size - great or small - but in the Nature of Quantity itself. So, there must be something that causes the Units (μονάδες, monades) to Move. And if it is the Life-Principle that causes Motion both in Living-Things and in Number, then the Life-Principle is Not both Mover and Moved - but only the Mover. But then, how could any one of these Units be this Mover? It must differ somehow from the rest. And what kind of difference could a Point (στιγμή, stigmē) have, except in terms of Position? If Units in the Body are distinct from Points, they would still occupy the same Place - for a Unit would lie in the position of a Point. But what would prevent many Units - even an infinite number - from occupying the same Place? Where there is no Division in Space, there cannot be any Division among these either. And if the Points in the Body are the Number that makes up the Life-Principle - or if the Life-Principle is the Number derived from the Body's Points - then why don't all Bodies have a Life-Principle? For every Body seems to contain Points - and in infinite number. And finally, how could these Points ever be separated from the Body - if even Lines cannot be divided into Points?

5: Rejecting Compositions of Bodies and Elements

It follows, as we have said before, that those who declare the Life-Principle to be identical with some fine-grained body fall into contradiction - especially thinkers like Democritus, who claims that the Living-Composite is Moved by the Life-Principle. For if the Life-Principle is indeed present in every Apprehending-Body (αἰσθανόμενον σῶμα), then there must be two Bodies occupying the same place - if the Life-Principle itself is also a Body. And for those who assert that it is a Number - if, for instance, in one Point there are many such Numerical Points - then either every Body would possess a Life-Principle, unless some distinct Number were added to the already-existing Points in that Body. The result would be that the Living-Composite is Moved by Number, just as Democritus claimed: for what difference would it make whether one speaks of tiny spheres or of large monads - or even simply of monads in Motion? In either case, the Living-Composite would necessarily be Moved insofar as those Elements are Moved. So, for those who attempt to fuse Motion and Number into one Structural-Account, all these contradictions arise - along with many others. Such a Definition of the Life-Principle is not only impossible; it collapses into absurdity. And the absurdity becomes even clearer when one attempts, from within this framework, to account for the Affections and

Functions of the Life-Principle - such as Reasoning, Apprehension, Pleasure, Pain, and all other Experiences. As we have already said, even guessing at their Nature on that basis would be no easy task.

Now, of the three traditional paths for defining the Life-Principle, some have declared it to be the Most-Mobile thing, because it Moves itself, others have claimed it to be the Finest-Kind of Body, or even the Most Not-Body compared to all others. We have already examined many of the contradictions in these views. What remains is to consider the claim that the Life-Principle is Composed from the Elements. For these thinkers argue that the Life-Principle Apprehends all Beings and recognizes each one individually. Thus, they say, it must be Composed of the same Elements as the things it Apprehends - on the principle that "like knows like." But in that case, many further impossibilities must follow. There are far more things - perhaps even an infinite number - that would have to be included within the Life-Principle if this Account were True. Suppose, then, that from the same Elements from which each of those things is Composed, the Life-Principle and the Capacity for Sense-Apprehension are likewise Formed. But then - what will Apprehend the Whole? What will recognize Composite-Beings like "Human," "God," "Flesh," or "Bone"? For it is not merely the Elements that make something exist as a Being - it is also Structured-

Narrative (λόγος) and Compositional-Unity (σύνθεσις), just as Empedocles says of bone:

> Earth, moistened in the hollow channels of the breast, won two parts out of eight of shining marrow; and four from Hephaestus - the white bones were born.

There would be no benefit in having the Elements within the Life-Principle unless the Accounts and Combinations that give form to Composites were present as well. For it is only through these that Beings like Bone or Human are Knowable. Without those, such recognition is impossible. And to say that this is impossible scarcely needs argument - for who would seriously claim that there is a stone or a human within the Life-Principle? The same reasoning applies to the Good and the Not-Good - and, indeed, to all other kinds of Beings. Since Being is said in many ways - signifying, for example, this particular thing, or quantity, or quality, or some other of the divided Categories - shall we then say that the Life-Principle is Composed of the Elements of all these? But it does not appear that all these Categories share common Elements. Shall we say instead that only Substances (οὐσίαι) are made from Elements? But then, how does the Life-Principle recognize the other kinds? Must we then claim that for each Category there are distinct Elements and unique Principles, from which the Life-Principle is

Composed? Then the Life-Principle would simultaneously be Quantity, Quality, and Substance. Yet it is absurd to suppose that something composed of the Elements of Quantity would be a Substance and yet not itself Quantity. Therefore, for those who say the Life-Principle is Composed of all things, all these absurdities follow.

Another contradiction arises from claiming that "Like is Not-Affected by Like," while also insisting that "Like Apprehends Like." For to Apprehend is to be Affected in some way - and to be Moved. The same is true of Thought-Apprehension (νοεῖν) and of Recognition (γινώσκειν). So many confusions and difficulties emerge from this way of speaking - as with Empedocles, who claims that all things are Recognized through Bodily Elements and by reference to the similar. But the point just made confirms the flaw: for all those parts of animal bodies composed solely of earth - like bones, sinews, and hair - seem entirely without Apprehension, and thus unable to Apprehend even those things that are like themselves. And yet, if the theory were True, they ought to. Moreover, for each supposed Elemental-Principle, ignorance would exceed Recognition. For even if the Life-Principle were able to Apprehend a given thing, it would necessarily remain ignorant of many others - indeed, of all the rest. In Empedocles' case, the god turns out to be the most ignorant of all. For of all the Elements, he fails to recognize one - Strife - while he recognizes all mortal things, since each of them is Composed of all the Elements. More broadly still - if every Being is either an Element or Composed of one or more or all of them, why is it that not all Beings possess a Life-Principle? For necessarily, if the Life-Principle is to recognize even a single thing - or a few, or all - then it must contain something corresponding to that thing, or to all of them. Yet here too arises the aporia: What-is-It that Unifies all these things? For the Elements themselves Appear more like Material-Stuff than anything else. The Essential-Factor seems to be that which binds them together - whatever that might be. But that anything should be greater than, or rule over, the Life-Principle is impossible. And even more impossible still would be something greater than Mind. For it is fitting that Mind is by Nature prior and sovereign in Essence. Yet these thinkers claim that the Elements are the First of all Beings.

All who assert that the Life-Principle is Composed of Elements - whether because of its Capacity to Recognize and Apprehend, or because it is said to be the Most-Mobile of things - fall into contradiction. For not all things that possess Apprehension are Mobile. There seem to be Living-Composites (ζῷα) which are fixed entirely in place. And yet it seems that only this kind of Motion - that initiated by the Life-Principle - produces the Motion of the Living-Composite. Likewise, those who derive both Mind and the Sense-Capacity (αἰσθητικόν) from the Elements are refuted. For it seems that plants are alive, and yet lack both the Capacity for Motion and for Apprehension. And many animals seem to lack Thought-Apprehension (διάνοια). Even if one were to grant this - and say that Mind is a Capacity of the Life-Principle, and likewise Apprehension - still, one could not rightly say this of every form of Life-Principle, nor of the whole, nor even of any single Unified-Form. This same confusion is found in the so-called Orphic Verses. There it is claimed that the Life-Principle enters the Body through Inhalation, borne on the winds. But this cannot apply to plants - or even to many animals - if not all beings inhale. And this flaw was overlooked by those who adopted such Accounts. Even if one concedes that the Life-Principle is Composed of the Elements, it is unnecessary for it to contain all of them. For a single half of any Opposition suffices to Apprehend both itself and its Opposite. We Apprehend both the Straight and the Curved by means of the Standard (κανών) - yet the Curved cannot judge either itself or the Straight. Some also say that the Life-Principle is Mixed throughout the Whole. Perhaps for this reason Thales imagined that all things are full of gods. But this account also produces aporiai: Why-is-it that the Life-Principle, when present in Air or Fire, does not produce a Living-Composite - while in Mixed-Bodies it does? And how could it be better in such Bodies - if it appears superior in the others? One might also ask why the Life-Principle existing in Air should be regarded as better or more immortal than that within animals. Either view leads to contradiction. For it would be even more absurd to call Fire or Air a Living-Composite than to deny that a Body which contains a Life-Principle is alive. These thinkers seem to reason that the Life-Principle is present in such substances because the Whole is homogeneous with its Parts. Thus, they are compelled to say that the Life-Principle, too, is homogeneous with its Parts - if it is by separating some portion of the surrounding Medium that a Living-Composite becomes an Ensouled-Body. But if Air, when divided, remains homogeneous, while the Life-Principle is not homogeneous, then it follows that Part of the Life-Principle may be present, while another Part may not. So it must be the case: either the Life-Principle is homogeneous in kind - of the same Nature throughout - or it is Not-Present in each Part of the Whole at all. From what has been said, it becomes evident that Recognition does not belong to the Life-Principle simply because it is Composed of Elements; nor can Motion rightly be Attributed to it on that basis. Since Recognition belongs to the Life-Principle - as do Apprehension, forming Opinions, Desire, Choice, and all Impulses (ὀρέξεις); and since Motion in Space, as well as Growth, Maturity, and Decay, are also produced by the Life-Principle - we must ask: do all these Functions belong to the entire Life-Principle? Do we think and Apprehend with the Whole, and likewise perform and undergo all other Activities? Or do different Parts of the Life-Principle perform different Functions? And what of Living itself? Does it belong to only one of these Capacities, or to several, or to all of them? Or does it Originate from something else entirely? Some have claimed that the Life-Principle is divisible - so that with one Capacity it Thinks, and with another it Desires. But if the Life-Principle is divisible by Nature, what holds it together? Surely not the Body - for it seems more likely that the Life-Principle holds the Body together. For when it departs, the Body dissolves and decays. So, if something else causes the Life-Principle to be Unified, then that something would most truly be the Life-Principle. But again, we must ask: is that Unifying thing one, or is it also divided into Parts? If it is one, then why not say that the Life-Principle is simply One? But if it is divided, we must again ask: what Unites that? - and so the Reasoning continues without end. There is also the Puzzle about the Capacities of its Parts, each of which exists within the Body. If the entire Life-Principle holds the whole Body together, then each Part of the Life-Principle must hold together some corresponding Capacity of the Body. But that seems impossible. For what kind of Part - or in what way - could the Mind (νοῦς) hold anything together? This is not easy even to imagine. Yet plants appear to go on living even when cut - and so too do some insects. This suggests they still retain the same kind of Life-Principle, even if not the same number. Indeed, each divided Part seems to possess its own Sense-Apprehension and Move itself spatially for a time. And if these parts do not continue indefinitely, that is no great mystery - for they lack the Organs needed to preserve their Nature. Still, it must be that in each Part, all the aspects of the Life-Principle are somehow present. The Parts are of the same kind with one another and with the whole - not as entirely distinct beings, but as parts of a divisible whole. It seems, in fact, that the First Capacity present in plants is some Form of Life-Principle. For both animals and plants share in this Single-Kind. And this Form of Life-Principle may be separated from the Apprehending-Capacity - but Apprehension is never found without this vegetative form.

Book II: Life-Principle: A New Beginning

1: First Analogy (Hylomorphic)

Having examined what has been handed down, let us now begin anew, attempting to Grasp what the Life-Principle is and to Determine its most Universal-Account. Among Beings, Essence appears as a kind of Genus. Of this, one Part, that which is Not-Yet in itself a "This-Something," is what we call Matter (ὕλη, hylē). Another is the Form (εἶδος eidos), the Actualizing-Structure through which it becomes a "This." And, a third is the Composite. Matter is an indeterminate state of Unity Before-Being that has Capacity, while the Form is the Actualized-Unity (and this in two Modes: one as Knowledge, the other as Contemplation). Of all Essences, Bodies appear to be Primary. Among these, Natural-Bodies are First - for they alone hold the Capacity for Life. And by Life, we mean the Capacity for Self-Nourishment, Growth, and Decay. Wherever these are found, we say that there is a Life-Principle in Potentiality (δυνάμει, dynamei) rather than Actuality (ἐνεργείᾳ, energeiai) - like a Natural-Body impressed with Form, shaped like wax to receive its seal. Therefore, any Natural-Body that partakes in Life would be a kind of Essence - but an Essence of the Composite-Kind. Since it is such a Body - one that is Alive - it follows that the Natural-Life Body is not itself the Life-Principle. It is not that which is Form, but that which underlies as Matter. The Life-Principle, then, must be an Essence - specifically, the Actualized-Unity of a Natural-Life Body which possesses the Capacity for Life. But Essence, in its primary sense, is First-Actuality. Thus, the Life-Principle is the First-Actuality of such a Natural-Life Body. And this is said in two ways: one as Knowledge, the other as Contemplation. It is evident that it is the first of these - Knowledge - for in the presence of the Life-Principle there exist both Waking and Sleeping. These stand in relation as Contemplating does to simply Possessing: Waking is to Contemplating as Sleeping is to Having. But among these, Knowledge is prior, just as First-Actuality is prior to its own use. Therefore, the Life-Principle is the First-Actuality of a Natural-Life Body that possesses the Capacity for Life. Such a Natural-Life Body would be one that is Organ-Possessing - that is, Composed of Parts fitted for Life. (Even the Parts of plants are Organs, though simple: the leaf as a covering for the fruit, the outer skin as a sheath for the seed. The roots are analogous to the mouth, for both draw in Nourishment.) If we must name what is common to every Life-Principle, it would be this: the First-Actuality of a Natural-Life Body is Organ-Possessing. Therefore, we must not inquire whether the Life-Principle and the Natural-Life Body are one - any more than we ask whether the wax and its

Impressed-Shape are one. Or more generally, we do not ask this of the Matter of any thing and its Form - for that for which the Matter exists is Not-Separate from it in Being. For both Being and What-it-Is are said in many ways - but in the Primary sense, it is the First-Actuality that is Essence.

In general, then, we have said what the Life-Principle is: it is the Essence according to the Universal-Account. This is what it is for such a Natural-Life Body to be. Just as if an axe were a Natural-Life Body, then its Essence would be its "Axe-Nature" - that is, its Life-Principle. For once this is removed, it is no longer an axe, except in name. It becomes merely a piece of metal shaped like an axe. For the Essence and Account of such a Body is not the Life-Principle - because an axe does not have within itself the Source of Movement or Rest. The Life-Principle belongs to a Natural-Life Body precisely insofar as it is Alive, possessing this Inner-Source. The same Account applies to each Sense-Apprehension Organ. If the Eye were itself a Living-Composite, then Sight would be its Life-Principle - for Sight is the Essence of the Eye, according to its Proper-Account. The Eye is the Matter for Sight. And when Sight is no longer present, it is no longer truly an Eye - except in name only, as with a stone eye or a painted eye. So we must think of the entire Natural-Life Body in the same way. Just as a single Sense-Apprehension Capacity is to its Sense-

Apprehension Organ, so the whole Apprehending-Capacity is to the whole Natural-Life Body that is structured for Sense-Apprehension. But it is not every such Natural-Life Body that possesses the Life-Principle, only that which Actualizes it. Seed and fruit are Natural-Life Bodies only in Potentiality. Just as cutting and seeing are forms of Potentiality rather than Actuality, so too is Waking a kind of First-Actuality. But just as Sight is the Capacity of the Eye's Sense-Apprehension Organ, so too is the Life-Principle the First-Actuality of the entire Natural-Life Body. That Natural-Life Body exists in Potentiality; the Life-Principle brings it into Actualized-Unity. Just as in the Eye there are both Pupil and Sight, so too in the Living-Composite there are both Natural-Life Body and Life-Principle.

It is clear, then, that the Life-Principle is not separate from the Natural-Life Body - nor are those Sense-Apprehension Capacities that belong to it by Nature. For in some cases, the First-Actuality of a Sense-Apprehension Capacity is identical with the Capacity itself. In other cases, the relation may be otherwise - since some Sense-Apprehension Capacities are not the First-Actuality of any Natural-Life Body at all. And it still remains uncertain whether the Life-Principle relates to the Natural-Life Body as a sailor to a ship. Let this, then, be taken as the provisional schema and signature definition of the Life-Principle.

2: Ensouled Natural-Life Body (Potentiality)

Since clarity often comes through things that are more apparent - though less precise - we must again approach the Life-Principle in this way. The Structured-Account must not only express what the Life-Principle is, as most definitions aim to do, but must also contain the Cause - such that the Cause is present within the Account itself. For many existing definitions function like Conclusions, not Causes - for example, when someone says that squaring means producing a square equal to a given rectangle, that is the Outcome, not the Cause. But when one says it is the Discovery of a mean line, that reveals the Cause. So let us begin again from Origin-Principles.

What distinguishes the Ensouled-Body from the Not-Ensouled-Body is Life. Yet Life is spoken of in many ways - and even if just one among these is present (such as Thinking, Sense-Apprehension, Motion or Rest in place, or Change through Nourishment, Growth, or Decay), we say that the being Lives. Thus, all Growing-Things are said to Live - for they possess within themselves a Capacity and a source by which they Grow and Decay in opposite directions. They grow both upward and downward, and outward in all directions. So long as they take in Nourishment, they persist in Living. This Capacity - what we call the Nutritive-Capacity - can exist apart from the others, but the others cannot exist without it, at least among Mortal-Beings. This is evident in plants, which possess no other Capacities of the Life-Principle. Thus, the Capacity for Living through Nourishment belongs to all Living-Beings, but the designation Animal arises first from the presence of Sense-Apprehension. Even Beings that do not Move or change location - so long as they possess Sense-Apprehension - are called Animals, not merely Living. And among Sense-Apprehensions, Touch-Apprehension is the First to arise in all Animals. Just as the Nutritive-Capacity can exist without Touch, so too Touch can exist apart from the other Sense-Apprehensions. So we call Nutritive that Capacity which plants share. But all Animals appear to have the Capacity for Touch. The reason why these two Capacities often appear together will be clarified later. Let us affirm for now only this: the Life-Principle is the source and boundary of all these Capacities - Nutritive, Sense-Apprehensive, Deliberative, and Motive. Whether each of these is a Capacity of the Life-Principle, and whether they are distinct only in Structured-Account or also in Location, is sometimes clear, sometimes difficult to determine. For example, in plants, some Capacities seem divisible and able to survive in separation. This suggests that within each plant, there is a single First-Actuality of the Life-Principle, but potentially multiple such Capacities. Likewise in animals: when insects are cut in two, each half continues to live, showing both Sense-Apprehension and localized Motion - and if it has Sense-Apprehension, then also Imagination and Desire. For wherever there is Sense-Apprehension, there is Pleasure and Pain - and where these are present, Desire follows. As for the Capacity of Thinking and Theoretical-Apprehension, this remains uncertain. It may belong to a different kind of Life-Principle altogether - perhaps one that alone is separable, as something Eternal is from something Perishable. But for the remaining Capacities of the Life-Principle, it is clear from this that they are not separable - contrary to some claims. Yet they are distinct in Structured-Account. For it is one thing to Apprehend, another to form Opinions, and so with all the other functions. Moreover, some Living-Beings possess all these Capacities, others only some, and still others only one. This is what distinguishes Living-Beings. The cause of this difference must be sought later. A similar differentiation appears among Sense-Apprehensions: some Living-Beings possess them all; others only some; and some only one - the most necessary, Touch.

Now, just as we say we Know in two ways - sometimes referring to Knowledge, sometimes to the Life-Principle - so too we say we are healthy in two ways: either in the state of Health itself, or in reference to the part or whole of the Natural-Life Body. Of these, Knowledge and Health are both Actualizing-Structures and Structured-Accounts, and like the First-Actuality of that which is receptive. The one belongs to the Capacity for Knowing, the other to Health. For the power of things that cause change seems to dwell in that which is being shaped. The Life-Principle then, is that by which we Live, Apprehend, and Understand most Truly. It is, therefore, a kind of Structured-Account and Actualizing-Structure - not a Substrate or Material. Since Essence has three meanings - Matter, Form, and the Composite - then Matter is Capacity, and Form is First-Actuality. And since the Ensouled-Body is a Composite, the Natural-Life Body is not the First-Actuality of the Life-Principle. Rather, the Life-Principle is the First-Actuality of a certain kind of Natural-Life Body - that which is capable of being Alive in Potentiality.

Thus, those who say the Life-Principle is neither Body nor without Body are right. It is not a Body, but it belongs to a Body, and exists in a certain kind of Body. The earlier thinkers who merely "fitted" the Life-Principle into just any Body were mistaken - for not every Matter can receive just any Form. This fits with Reason: the First-Actuality of any Being belongs to what exists in Potentiality, in Matter appropriate to it. So it is evident from this that the Life-Principle is a kind of First-Actuality and Structured-Account of a Natural-Life Body capable of being Alive in Potentiality.

3: Life-Principle Living-Composite: Five Capacities

Among the Capacities of the Life-Principle, as previously stated, some Living-Composites possess them all, while others possess only a few - and some, only one. We have named these Capacities: Nutritive, Desire, Sense-Apprehension, Locomotive (by place), and Thinking. Plants possess only the Nutritive-Capacity. Other Living-Beings possess this as well as the Sense-Apprehension Capacity. But where Sense-Apprehension is present, Desire must also be. For Desire includes Appetite, Spirited-Impulse, and Deliberate-Wishing - and all Animals possess at least one Sense-Apprehension, namely Touch-Apprehension. Where Sense-Apprehension exists, so too do Pleasure and Pain - and thus, the Pleasant and the Painful. And wherever these are present, Desire necessarily follows - for Desire is directed toward the Pleasant. Furthermore, Animals possess Sense-Apprehension of Nourishment - for it is through Touch that Nourishment is Grasped. All Animals feed upon the dry and moist, the hot and the cold - and it is precisely these that Touch Grasps. The other Sense-Apprehendables - such as Sound, Color, and Smell - are sensed only incidentally, since they do not pertain to Nourishment. Flavor, however, belongs among the Tangible Sense-Apprehendables. Hunger and Thirst are themselves forms of Desire: Hunger for the dry and hot, Thirst for the cold and moist. Flavor, then, is a kind of Harmonious-Mixture of these. The precise Nature of this must be clarified later. For now, it is sufficient to note that every Animal possessing Touch also possesses Desire. Whether Imagination also belongs among these remains uncertain and must be investigated later.

Some Living-Beings, in addition to these Capacities, possess the Capacity for Locomotion. Others possess, beyond these, Thinking and Mind - such as humans, or whatever other Beings may be similar or superior. It is evident, then, that just as there could be a general Account of Shape applying to triangle and square alike - though not proper to any of them - so too there could be a general Structured-Account of the Life-Principle which applies to all types, but is not fully proper to any single one. One should not search for a common definition that fits both all figures and all Life-Principles, while abandoning the distinctive Structured-Account of each. For in both Domains - Figural and Vital - the earlier form exists in Potentiality within the later: the triangle within the square, the Nutritive-Capacity within the Sensitive. Therefore, in every Case, we must ask: What is the Life-Principle of this Being? Of the plant? Of the human? Of the beast? And why, in the order of Nature, does it unfold this way? The Sensitive cannot exist without the Nutritive - but the Nutritive can exist without the Sensitive, as seen in plants. Likewise, no complete Sense-Apprehension occurs without the full set of Sense-Apprehensions, but Touch can exist without the others.

Indeed, many animals lack sight, hearing, or even smell. Among sensing beings, some possess Locomotive, while others do not. And finally - rarest of all - some possess Reasoning and Thought. Those who can reason about Mortal-Things possess all the other Capacities as well. But those who possess only some of the others may lack Reason - and even Imagination. And some Live only through Imagination alone. As for the Contemplative-Mind, this must be addressed in another inquiry. For now, it is clear that the most fitting way to understand the Life-Principle is to give an Account of each Capacity individually.

4: Life-Principle is Cause and Origin-Principle

Anyone who intends to inquire into these matters must begin by clearly Grasping what each Capacity of the Life-Principle is - before proceeding to those that are interrelated, and then to all the rest. But if one must first define what each Capacity is - whether Form (νοητικόν), Sense (αἰσθητικόν), or Nutritive - then one must begin even earlier by stating what it means to Apprehend Form (νοεῖν), and what it means to Apprehend through Sense (αἰσθάνεσθαι). For Actualizations (ἐνέργειαι) and Activities (πράξεις) are, in Reason's order, prior to Capacities (δυνάμεις). And if that is so, then what precedes even these

- namely, the Objects they are directed toward - must be examined first. So it is appropriate to begin with these: Nourishment, the Apprehendable (αἰσθητόν), and the Intelligible (νοητόν). Let us begin, then, with Nourishment and Generation. The Nutritive-Capacity of the Life-Principle belongs not only to all the others but is also the First and most common of its Capacities through which all Living-Composites (ζῷα) are said to be Alive. The work of this Capacity is to generate and to make use of Nourishment. For this is the most Natural of all works belonging to Living-Beings: to bring into Being another of the same kind - plant from plant, animal from animal - so that each may share, to the extent possible, in the Eternal and the Divine. All things are oriented toward this; everything acts by Nature for-the-sake-of it. The 'For-the-Sake-of-Which' (οὗ ἕνεκα) is spoken of in two ways: as the End itself, and as that in which the End is achieved. Since no Perishable Thing can remain numerically identical while partaking continuously in the Eternal, each participates in it in the way that it can - some more, some less. And they persist not as the same in number, but as the same in Actualizing-Structure (εἶδος).

The Life-Principle, then, is the Cause (αἰτία) and Origin-

Principle (ἀρχή) of the Living-Composite Body. This is true in multiple senses. The Life-Principle is a Cause in all three ways: it is the Origin of Motion; it is that for-the-sake-of-which something Is; and it is the very Essence of the Living-Composite. That it is Essence is clear - for Essence is what makes a thing Be what it Is. And for Living-Beings, Being-Alive is their very Being - and this arises from the Life-Principle. Whatever exists only in Potentiality can be known only through reference to its Full-Realization - its Actualized-Unity (ἐντελέχεια). The Life-Principle is therefore also the Final-Cause, the that for-the-sake-of-which. Just as Mind (νοῦς) always acts for-the-sake-of some end, so too does Nature - and in the case of Living-Beings, the Life-Principle is the End, in accordance with Nature. All Natural-Life Bodies are instruments of the Life-Principle - both in animals and in plants - because they exist for-the-sake-of the Life-Principle. And this 'for-the-sake-of-which' is spoken of in both ways, as previously noted.

Now, the Capacity by which Locomotion arises is also derived from the Life-Principle, though not all Living-Beings possess it. So too are change in Quality and Growth derived from the Life-Principle. For Sense-Apprehension appears as a kind of Alteration, and nothing Apprehends unless it possesses a Life-Principle.

Likewise for Growth and Decay: for nothing Grows or Decays Naturally unless it is Nourished, and nothing is Nourished without partaking in Life. Empedocles did not speak well when he said that plants grow downward by the Nature of Earth and upward by the Nature of Fire. For he did not account properly for what "Up" and "Down" mean - for these are not the same in all things, nor in the Cosmos as a whole. Just as the head is "up" for animals, so the roots are "up" for plants. Therefore, the tools must be named according to the work they perform. Furthermore, what keeps Earth and Fire united, if they are by Nature carried in opposite directions? They would be torn apart unless held together by something. That "something" is the Life-Principle - the cause of both Growth and Nourishment. Some assert that Fire alone is the cause of Nourishment and Growth, since Fire seems to be the only Element or Body that grows and Nourishes itself. From this, one might suppose that Fire is the cause of these effects in both plants and animals. But Fire is only a co-Cause - not the primary or sufficient one. The greater Cause is the Life-Principle. Fire increases infinitely, so long as it has fuel - but for Natural-Composites, there is always a limit and a Rational-Account (λόγος) for both Quantity and Growth - and these arise not from Fire, but from the Life-Principle, and more from Reason than from Matter. Since the defining work of the Nutritive-Capacity is Nourishment and Generation, we must now define Nourishment. For it is this work that distinguishes this Capacity from the others. Nourishment seems to be contrary to that which it Nourishes - not in every respect, but among those contraries from which Generation and Growth arise. Many things come to be from opposites - but not everything that comes to be increases in Quantity. For instance, health may come from sickness, but it does not increase Quantity. Moreover, even in such transformations, the things do not Nourish one another equally. Water Nourishes Fire - but Fire does not Nourish Water. Among the simple Bodies, this relation appears most clearly: one thing Nourishes, another is Nourished. A difficulty arises here. Some claim that the Like is Nourished by the Like - since it grows by what is like it. Others, as we mentioned, claim the contrary: that the Unlike Nourishes the Unlike - for the Like cannot act upon the Like, while Nourishment must be transformed and digested, and all transformation goes toward the Contrary or the Intermediate. Indeed, Nourishment is affected by that which it Nourishes, but not vice versa. The Nourished is not acted upon by the Nourishment - any more than the builder is acted upon by the wood. Rather, Nourishment is acted upon by the Life-Principle, just as the builder acts upon the wood, moving from Potentiality into Activity. There is also ambiguity over whether Nourishment is what joins first or what is left last. If both, then in one sense it is undigested, in another digested - and in that case, we may use the term "Nourishment" for both Apprehensions. In its undigested form, it Nourishes as Contrary to Contrary. In its digested form, as Like to Like. So both Accounts are partly True and partly Incomplete. Since nothing is Nourished that does not share in Life, the Body that is Nourished must be an Ensouled-Body. Thus, Nourishment belongs to the Living-Composite as such, not merely by coincidence. There is a distinction between what is Nourishment and what is Growth-Producing. For the Ensouled-Body, as having Quantity, is the Agent of Growth; but as this particular Being, as Substance, it is what is Nourished. For Nourishment preserves the Substance, and it remains in Being only as long as it is Nourished. The Generative-Capacity of the Life-Principle does not Generate the very same Being that is Nourished, but rather something like it. For the Being that is Nourished is already a complete Substance, it does not Generate itself, but Preserves itself. Thus, the Nutritive-Capacity of the Life-Principle is that which Preserves the Being that possesses it in the kind of Being that it Is.

Nourishment enables its Activity. Without Nourishment, it cannot remain in Being. There are three elements in this process: that which is Nourished, that by which it is Nourished, and that which performs the

Nourishing. The Natural-Life Body is what is Nourished; Nourishment is that by which; and the Life-Principle, in virtue of the Nutritive-Capacity, is that which performs the Nourishing. And since everything is rightly named by its End - and the End here is the Generation of another like itself, the Nutritive-Capacity, which is the First and most common of all the Capacities of the Life-Principle, may rightly be called the Generative-Capacity of the same. Just as in steering, there are two tools - the hand and the rudder: one Moving and Moved, the other moving but not Moved - so too, in Nourishment, there is a duality. All Nourishment must be digestible, and the cause of digestion is Heat. Therefore, every Living-Composite contains Heat. Thus, in outline, we have said what Nourishment is. Its fuller treatment must be taken up later, in its proper context.

5: Sense-Capacity and Actualized Object

Now that each of the particular Sense-Capacities has been distinguished, we must speak more generally about Sense-Apprehension. As previously established, Sense-Apprehension always involves being Moved and Affected - it appears to be a kind of Alteration (ἀλλοίωσις).

Some have claimed that one Like-Thing can be affected by another Like-Thing - but whether that is possible or impossible has already been considered in our earlier inquiry into Acting and being Acted-Upon. A difficulty arises here: Why is it that we do not Apprehend the Apprehensions themselves? Why is there no Sense-Apprehension of Sense-Apprehension? Why also do Apprehensions not occur when no external Apprehendables are present - even though the Elemental-Constituents (such as fire and earth) are already within the Natural-Life Body? Does Sense-Apprehension arise from those Elemental-Parts themselves, or from some Incidental-Configuration that they compose? It becomes evident that the Sense-Capacity does not Actualize itself, but only exists in Potentiality. Just as a flammable object does not burn of its own accord - for if it could, it would ignite itself and not require external Fire - so too the Sense-Capacity requires something already Actualized to bring it into activity. We use the term "Sense-Apprehension" in two ways - we may call one a hearer or seer simply for having the Capacity (even when asleep), but we also apply these terms when someone is actively Apprehending. Thus, Sense-Apprehension is spoken of both in Potentiality and in Actualized-Unity. Let us then clarify: Being-Moved, Being-Affected, and Being-Actualized can all refer to the same phenomenon. Motion, in a way, is a kind of Actualization - though an incomplete one, as discussed elsewhere. Anything that is Affected or Moved is Acted-Upon by something already Actualized and capable of producing Effect. Thus, one might say the Sense-

Capacity is affected by something either Similar or Not-Similar to itself. As previously stated: the Not-Like is what undergoes Affection, but once Affected, it becomes Like.

We must now distinguish more precisely between Potentiality and Actualized-Unity, since our earlier usage was loose. For instance, we may call someone a "Knower" simply because they are Human - since the Human-Kind possesses the Capacity for Knowledge. But we also call someone a "Knower" if they have actually acquired a discipline such as grammar. These are not the same. The first is Potentiality in-kind, the second is Potentiality with acquired possession. Both are Potential Knowers - but in distinct ways. One has the Natural constitution to become a Knower; the other already possesses the Knowledge and only needs the Will to Contemplate (φρόνησις) - unless hindered by something external. One

who is Contemplating is, in the strictest sense, a Knower-in-Actualization. Thus, the first becomes a Knower-through-Habituation - by repeated transformations through exposure to contraries. The second already possesses Knowledge, even if not actively using it - so one may still not be Acting, despite having the Capacity.

Now, Being-Affected (πάσχειν) is not one single kind. In one sense, it is destruction by an opposite; in another, it is the fulfillment of Potentiality when joined with something Actualized and like in kind. The Knower becomes a Contemplator not by being destroyed or reshaped, but by becoming what he already is in fuller measure. Either this is not Alteration at all, or it is a distinct kind. Thus, it is not accurate to say that the Thinker is altered while Thinking - any more than the Builder is altered while Building. The Movement from Potentiality to Actualization, in the case of Contemplation, should not be called instruction or alteration at all. By contrast, to be Moved toward Knowledge through learning is something different: either not an affection, or a distinct kind - one that transforms toward completion rather than decay. In Sense-Apprehension, the initial Actualization comes from the agent that triggers it. Once this is complete, the Sense-Capacity possesses something like Knowledge. In this respect, the activity of Sense-Apprehension resembles the activity of Contemplation. Yet there is a distinction: Contemplation arises from within, while Sense-Apprehension always requires something external - such as a Visible or Audible object. The same holds true for the other Sense-Capacities. This explains why Sense-Apprehension pertains to particular External-Things, while Knowledge pertains to universal Forms. Still, both reside in the Life-Principle. One may Think or Contemplate at will - but one cannot simply Grasp Apprehendables by willing it. For the Perceptible must already be present. The same applies to recalling Sense-Objects: we cannot remember them simply by choosing to, if the Objects themselves are absent. This is because Sense-Objects are external and particular. These matters require fuller discussion elsewhere. But for now, let this be settled - when something is said to be in Potentiality, this may mean either, as when a child is said to be "capable of command," or as when an adult is said to be so. The Sense-Capacity belongs to the latter. We lack precise names for these distinctions, though we have now clarified them both in Account and by differentiation. Thus, we are compelled to speak of "Being-Affected" and "Being-Altered" as our default expressions. The Sense-Capacity, then, in Potentiality, becomes like the Apprehendable Object when that Object is Present in Actualization. And as said before: the Sense-Capacity is not initially like the Object it apprehends, but becomes like it through Affection.

6: Natural Proper-Apprehendables

Let us now speak, for each Sense-Capacity individually, about the Apprehendable Objects, beginning from the fundamental distinctions. These Apprehendables are said to be of three kinds: two are Apprehended in themselves, one is Apprehended incidentally. Of the two Apprehended in themselves, one is Proper to each individual Sense-Capacity; the other is common to all. By Proper (ἴδιον), I mean what belongs uniquely to a single Sense-Capacity, and cannot be Not-Apprehended with respect to what it is - for example: Color for Sight, Sound for Hearing, and Flavor for Taste. Touch encompasses many types of difference, but still, each type is Apprehended by a tactile sense in a way that does not confuse it with another - no one mistakes a Texture for a Color or a Sound. These, then, are called Proper-Apprehendables (ἴδια αἰσθητά): each one tied specifically to a single Sense-Capacity. In contrast, the Common-Apprehendables (κοινὰ αἰσθητά) are such things as Motion, Rest, Number, Shape, and Size. These are not Proper to any one Sense-Capacity but are Apprehended by all of them together. For instance, Motion may be Apprehended both by Sight and by Touch. The third kind of Apprehendable is that which is Apprehended Incidentally (κατὰ συμβεβηκός). For example: one sees something white and says, "That is the son of Diares." Here, it is not the "son of Diares" that the Sense-Capacity Apprehends, but merely the white thing. That incidental identity comes through Association - not through direct Apprehension. Therefore, the Sense-Capacity is not affected by the Incidental Quality itself, but only by the Apprehendable that directly presents itself. Among the things Apprehended in themselves, the Proper-

Apprehendables are the most strictly and truly Perceptible. Each Sense-Capacity is Naturally configured to Apprehend its own Proper-Apprehendables - these are the very things for the sake of which that specific Sense-Apprehension exists.

7. Sight and Transparent Mediums

Wherever Sight-Apprehension exists, there must also be the Visible (ὁρατόν). The Visible consists first and foremost of Color (χρῶμα), and also of something that can be named by Reason, though there is no commonly agreed term for it. This unnamed aspect will become clearer as we proceed.Color is the Proper-Apprehendable of Sight - it is that which is in itself Visible. And this is not merely a definitional claim, but an essential one: it is Visible because it inherently possesses the Capacity to activate the transparent Medium in Actualization (διαφανές κατ' ἐνέργειαν) - and that is its Nature. Therefore, nothing is seen apart from Light (φῶς), since all colors appear within Light. So let us first explain what Light is. There exists something we call the Transparent (διαφανές): that which is Visible not by itself but through another, namely, through what gives it Color. Air, water, and many solids are Transparent - not because of their substance, but because of a shared

Nature of Transparency they possess, which is also present in the Celestial-Body. Light is the Actualization - the Potentiality, now in Actualization, of this Transparent Medium when it is brought into activity by Fire, or something similar (such as the Celestial-Element). Light is therefore not a body, nor an emission from a body - it is the Active-Presence of Fire or something like it in the Transparent. This presence Actualizes the Transparent - Darkness (σκότος) is the Not-Actualization of the Transparent. Thus, Empedocles and others who claim that Light travels across space and reaches Earth in some time-delayed way are mistaken. That claim contradicts both Reason and the evidence of Sense-Apprehension: for such travel would seem either too quick at small distances or too slow across vast spaces. That which receives Color must itself be Not-Color (ἄχρουν) - just as that which receives Sound must be Not-Sound (ἄψοφον).

So too the Transparent is Not-Color - not inherently Not-Visible, but Not-Visible when it is in Potentiality rather than Actualization. The same Transparent-Capacity is sometimes Darkness and sometimes Light, depending on whether it is Potential or Actual. All Visible things appear in Light - but only the Proper-Color of each Object is truly seen in Light. Some things appear to shine even in darkness (like glowing fungi or fish scales), but what we see is not their Proper-Color. Such phenomena - fiery or luminous - form a separate Category, whose cause must be discussed later. For now, it is enough to understand this: Color is seen only in Light. That is, Color becomes Visible because it activates the Transparent, which in turn activates the Sense-Organ. And Light is the Transparent in Actualization. This is confirmed by experience: if a colored Object is placed directly on the eye, it is not seen. It is the Medium, such as Air, that is first affected - and because it is continuous, it transmits the Motion to the Sense-Organ. Democritus was correct about this: if there were a void between Object and eye, nothing would be seen - not even the tiniest object suspended in the sky. For Sight requires that the Sense-Capacity be affected - not by direct contact with the Color (which cannot touch), but through the Medium. If the Medium were absent (as in a void), vision would not merely be distorted - it would not happen at all. Hence, Color is seen only through Light, by way of the Medium. Fire, however, can be seen in both Light and darkness, because Fire itself Actualizes the Transparent.

The same holds true for Sound and Smell: these do not reach the Sense-Organ by direct contact. Instead, the Medium between the Object and the Organ is Moved first, and this motion is then transmitted to the organ. If the Sound-Producing or Odor-Producing Object were pressed directly against the ear or the nose, no

Apprehension would occur. Even in Touch and Taste, the same principle holds - though it is not immediately obvious. This will be clarified later. In all cases, there must be a Medium between the Apprehendable and the Apprehender. For Sound, this Medium is Air. For Smell, the Medium has no special name - but it is clearly something common to Air and Water, just as the Transparent is common to both, and to the Heavens. Animals that live in water also possess the Sense-Apprehension of Smell. As for land-dwelling animals who breathe, especially humans, it is not possible to smell without breathing. The reason for this, too, will be explained in what follows.

8: Sound and Hearing, Voice, and Breathing

Let us first make distinctions concerning Sound (ψόφος, psophos) and Hearing (ἀκοή, akoē). Sound is twofold: in one sense, it is an Actualization, and in another, a Potentiality. We say that some things do not have sound - such as sponges or wool - while others do, such as bronze or anything solid and smooth, because these are capable of producing sound. That Capacity consists in being able to produce sound in Actualization, in the region between the sounding Object and the hearing-organ. Sound in Actualization always arises from something acting on something else and within some Medium. For it is a blow (πληγή, plēgē) that causes sound

- and a blow cannot occur from only one thing. There must be both what strikes and what is struck. Thus, anything that sounds does so in relation - it is a toward-something motion. Now a blow cannot happen without Motion. But not every blow produces Sound. Wool, even when struck, does not sound; but bronze does - and hollow objects as well. Bronze sounds because it is solid and smooth; hollow things because the rebound of air inside produces many sequential blows after the first, as the disturbed air cannot escape all at once. Sound is Apprehended in both air and water, though less clearly in water. But air and water are not themselves the source of Sound. Rather, there must be a blow from solid objects - against each other and against the air. This happens when the air is struck and cannot immediately disperse. Therefore, if the blow is quick and forceful, the motion must be faster than the dispersal of air - just as if one were striking swiftly-moving sand. Sound is also produced when air, enclosed in a vessel and made continuous, is compressed and then rebounded like a ball. There always seems to be an echo, but not a clear one. This is analogous to what happens in Light. Light is always reflected, otherwise there would be no darkness beyond the sun's path. But this reflection does not occur in the same way as from water or bronze or other smooth surfaces that cast shadows by which we judge the presence of Light. Likewise in Sound: the boundary of its effect is not always clearly marked. It is rightly said that the void - or seeming void - is the Medium of Hearing. Air seems empty, and it is air that enables Hearing when Moved in a continuous and bounded way toward the hearing-organ. Hearing is tied to air. When the outer-air is Moved, the inner-air is also Moved. Hence, not every animal hears - because not every animal has air distributed throughout the body. Nor is every part of the Body an Ensouled-Body (ἔμψυχον). Air itself is silent by Nature, because of its fragility. But when its dispersal is blocked, the Motion it undergoes becomes Sound. The Structure of the ear has been designed to remain still, so that it can clearly Grasp all changes in the Motion of Graspable Apprehendables. This is also why hearing is possible in water: the outer-air does not enter the ear directly - nor even into the spiral interior - so if this structure is damaged, hearing ceases, just as damage to the pupil membrane impairs vision. A sign of Hearing (or not) is that the ear always rings, like a horn. The air inside is always moving in a native way. But the Sound proper to Apprehension is foreign - not one's own. That is why people say we hear through a void or through what is sounding - because Hearing occurs in air that has been given Form and boundedness. Now, whether Sound is produced by the struck or the striker, or both in different ways, it is best to say that Sound is a kind of Motion that can be received in a certain way - like a rebound from a smooth surface. Not everything that strikes sounds; nor does everything that is struck. Two needles striking make no sound. The struck Object must be smooth - so that air may gather, rebound, and vibrate. Pitch differences arise from Actualized Sound. Just as there is no Apprehension of Color without Light, so too there is no Apprehension of high or low pitch - those Graspable Apprehendables - without Sound. These names - high (ὀξύ) and low (βαρύ) - are metaphorical, borrowed from Touch. High-pitched Sound Moves the sense quickly in a narrow range; low-pitched Moves it slowly across a broad span. The distinction lies not in speed but in the mode of Motion and the range of contact. The sharp (ὀξύ) is like something that pierces; the blunt (ἀμβλύ) is like something that presses. The one acts in a small range, the other in a wide range. Therefore, sharp seems fast, blunt seems slow. Let this be our account of Sound.

Now we turn to Voice (φωνή, phōnē). Voice is a type of Sound that belongs to an Ensouled-Body. Not-Animate things do not have Voice. When we say a flute or lyre "has voice," this is metaphorical. These instruments produce stretch, tone, and articulation - but without Life-Principle. Voice has these too, but many animals - even those with blood - do not have Voice. Fish, for example.

This is reasonable, if Voice is a kind of Air-Motion. Animals that breathe use air for two things - like the tongue for tasting and for speaking. Tasting is necessary; speaking is for Excellence.

So too with Breathing: it serves both inner-heat and Voice. The explanation for this belongs to another inquiry. But for Voice to exist, it must involve Breath. The pharynx is the instrument; the lungs are the region - especially in land animals, where the lungs are warmest. The region around the heart is the first to require breath. Hence, it is necessary for Air to be drawn inward in Breathing. Voice arises when the breathed air is struck by the Life-Principle at work in this region - near the so-called artery. Not every sound from an animal is Voice. One may make a noise with the tongue - like a cough - but this is not Voice. Voice must come from a Living-Being with Imagination (φαντασία, phantasia), and it must be signifying. Voice is not merely the sound of exhaled air (as in coughing); it arises when that air strikes the artery with intent. A sign of this is that those who do not inhale or exhale cannot speak. It is when the air is held and directed that it can cause Motion. This is also why fish are voiceless: they have no pharynx, they do not take in air, they do not breathe. The cause of this is for another inquiry.

9:

Smell (ὀσμή, osmē) and the organ responsible for its Sense-Apprehension (ὀσφραντικόν, osphrantikon) are more obscure than the other Apprehensions. Unlike Sound or Color, it is not immediately clear what kind of Being Smell is. This difficulty arises because human beings possess a weak Sense-Apprehension of Smell. They do not clearly Grasp odors unless accompanied by something pleasant or painful. This reveals that the organ of Sense-Apprehension for Smell in humans is imprecise. It is much like animals whose eyes are covered or dense: such beings can apprehend Color, but not with accuracy - only in terms of what is frightening or not. In this same way, human Smell-Apprehension is dulled and indistinct. Still, Smell seems analogous to Taste.

The kinds of smells resemble kinds of flavors. However, human beings have a clearer Apprehension of Taste because Taste is a kind of Touch - and Touch is the most accurate of all the Sense-Apprehension Capacities in humans. Although humans are inferior to many animals in most other Apprehensions, in Touch-Apprehension they excel. For this reason, humans are also the most intelligent of animals. This is demonstrated by the fact that, even within the human species, the precision of the Touch-Organ corresponds with intelligence. Those with firm, dense flesh are dull-minded in Apprehension; those with soft flesh are quick-witted in Apprehension.

Just as Flavors are sweet or bitter, so too are Smells. Some smells correspond directly to flavors (such as a sweet smell with a sweet flavor), while others are opposites. There are also smells that are sharp, dry, pungent, or oily. But because Smell-Apprehension is less precise than Taste-Apprehension, we use names for smells borrowed from the more familiar realm of flavor. Thus, a sweet smell is called "honey-like" or "saffron-like"; a pungent smell is called "thyme-like" or "garlic-like." This naming by resemblance is common across the senses.

As with every other Apprehension, Smell operates through opposites. Hearing discerns what is audible and inaudible; sight, what is Visible and invisible. Smell discerns what is smellable and what is Un-Smellable. What is completely incapable of producing smell is called Un-Smellable in the strictest sense; what produces a minimal or indistinct odor is also called Un-Smellable, but in a weaker sense. A parallel holds in Taste: what is completely flavorless is Un-Tastable; what produces only a faint taste is also said to be Un-Tastable, but differently.

Smell, like all the other Apprehensions, occurs through a Medium - either Air or water. Aquatic animals appear capable of smelling, just as do those who live in Air - whether blooded or not. In both environments, some smells are apprehended from a distance, especially those connected with Nourishment. This raises a question: Why do human beings need to inhale (ἀναπνοή, anapnoē) in order to smell, while other animals do not? For when humans exhale or hold their breath, they cannot Grasp odors - not from far away, not up close, not even when the source is placed directly at the nostrils.

The fact that something can touch the Sense-Apprehension Organ and still not be Apprehended is common to all the Apprehensions. But that humans cannot smell without inhaling is unique to them - and clearly confirmed by experience. If there are animals that smell but do not breathe, then the structure of their Smell-Apprehension must differ in mechanism, even if it is aligned with the same function: the Apprehension of what is fragrant or foul. Also, strong smells - such as those from asphalt or sulfur - harm the Smell-Apprehension Organ in both humans and animals. This shows that Smell-Apprehension does not require inhalation in itself. Rather, human beings require it because the structure of their organ is different - just as the eye differs between animals. Some animals have uncovered eyes, allowing them to see without obstruction; humans, by contrast, have eyelids, which must be opened to see. Similarly, some animals have exposed smell-organs; others (like humans) have covered organs. For humans, inhalation serves to uncover the organ by pulling Air inward.

This process opens the pores and vessels necessary for Smell-Apprehension. For this reason, animals that breathe cannot smell underwater - inhalation does not happen in a liquid medium. Smell relates to dryness, just as Taste relates to moisture. The organ of Smell is structured to receive dryness in Potentiality.

10: Taste

The Tasteable (γευστόν, geuston) is a kind of Touchable (ἁπτόν, hapton). Because of this, it cannot be Grasped through an external Medium that is Alien (ἀλλότριον μέσον, allotrion meson) - that is, foreign to the sensing body. Even Touch-Apprehension itself does not operate through such a separate Medium. The substance in which the Flavor-Element (χυμός, chymos) is present - the Tasteable - is some sort of fluid Body-Type, which is by Nature Touchable. For this reason, even if we were submerged in water, we would still Grasp sweetness - not through the water as Medium, but because the sweet substance intermixes with the fluid already within the body, just as happens in drinking. In contrast, we do not see Color by way of mixture or efflux. Just as the Medium in Sight-Apprehension is transparent and not itself

Visible, and Color is what is in-itself Visible, so too the Flavor-Element is that which is in-itself Tasteable.

There is no Grasping of the Flavor-Element without moisture - not merely in Potentiality but in Actuality. For example, the salty dissolves easily in moisture and can act directly upon the tongue. Just as Sight-Apprehension Grasp both what is Visible and what is Invisible - darkness being not-visible, yet still Grasped - and even that which is blinding, like excessive light - so too does Hearing-Apprehension grasp both Sound and Silence. Silence is inaudible, yet still apprehended as such. Likewise, overwhelming Sound, like blinding brightness, is Grasped in a different mode. A very soft Sound may be inaudible in one way; an excessively loud or violent Sound in another.

In all these Apprehensions, "Not-Visible" or "Not-Audible" may refer either to that which is utterly un-Graspable or to that which is defectively structured - like a footless animal or a seedless fruit. The same holds for Taste-Apprehension: it Grasp both the Tasteable and the Tasteless. Something may be Tasteless because it contains only a faint or degraded Flavor-Element, or because it harms the Taste-Apprehension Organ. The primary division between Drinkable and Un-Drinkable fluids appears to be the beginning of all Taste-Grasping. Both are apprehended, but the Un-Drinkable damages the organ, while the Drinkable is its proper Object.

Drinkability lies at the intersection of Touch and Taste, since all Tasteables are fluid substances. For this reason, the Taste-Apprehension Organ cannot itself be moist in Actuality, nor utterly dry. It must be Potentially Moist - capable of being made moist without being already so - and it must remain intact as it undergoes the change caused by contact with the Tasteable. A clear sign of this: the tongue cannot Grasp Apprehendables if it is either too dry or overly saturated. It must contact the initial moisture of the Flavor-Element directly. This is apparent when one tastes a strong Flavor-Element, then immediately another - the tongue retains some moisture from the first. Similarly, those who are ill Grasp all Flavor-Elements as bitter, because their tongues are saturated with pathological moisture, and all subsequent Taste-Grasping passes through that condition.

The kinds of Flavor-Elements, like Colors, follow a range structured by opposition. Sweet and Bitter form the most fundamental pair. After Sweetness comes the Oily, and after Bitterness, the Salty. Between these lie the Sharp, Astringent, Pungent, and Sour. These appear to make up the primary differentiations among Flavor-Elements. Thus, the Taste-Apprehension Organ exists in Potentiality, and the Tasteable Actualizes the Grasp in Actuality.

11: Touch

The Account of the Touchable and of Touch-Apprehension is one and the same. If Touch-Apprehension is not a single mode but rather many, then the Touchables must also differ in kind. This raises a puzzle: Are the kinds of Touchables one or many? And what is, in truth, the Sense-Apprehension Organ for Touch? Is it the flesh, or its analogue in other animals, or is that merely a Medium, with the true Primary-Organ lying within?

Each Sense-Apprehension corresponds to a basic Opposition: Sight to white and black, Hearing to high and low pitch, Taste to sweet and bitter. But Touch-Apprehension seems to grasp many oppositions - hot and cold, dry and moist, hard and soft, and others like them. Yet even in the other Apprehensions, more than one Opposition is present. In Sound, there are not only sharp and flat, but also loud and soft, smooth and rough. In Color, too, the oppositions extend beyond light and dark.

Still, what is the single underlying Element that plays the role in Touch-Apprehension that Color plays in Sight-Apprehension, or Sound in Hearing? That remains obscure. Is the Sense-Apprehension Organ for Touch internal, or is it simply the flesh? The immediacy of Apprehension upon contact with flesh does not prove the flesh is the true Organ. For example, if the flesh were wrapped in a membrane and we still apprehended through it, the result would be the same. And if the membrane were fused to the flesh, the Apprehension would be even quicker. This suggests that the flesh acts like a surrounding Medium. Just as if we were surrounded by Air, we might mistakenly think we grasp Color, Sound, and Smell through a single Medium, and so misidentify the kinds of Apprehension. But since each Apprehension has its own pathway, we know their Organs must be distinct.

In Touch-Apprehension, the distinction is not as evident. The Ensouled-Body cannot consist entirely of Air or Water, as such Elements lack the required solidity. It must be a composite, involving Earth, as the Nature of flesh suggests. The Ensouled-Body is thus the Medium in contact with the Touchable, and it is through this that the many kinds of Touch-Apprehension occur. The evidence: the tongue apprehends all kinds of Touchables and also Flavor-Elements. If the rest of the flesh also apprehended Flavor-Elements, then Touch-Apprehension and Taste-Apprehension would be the same. But they are distinct, because they do not function interchangeably. One may ask: If every body has depth, and if there is always something between two bodies, how can one ever truly Touch another?

The Ensouled-Body is always accompanied by moisture. Even what flows must be water, or contain water. So in Water, any two objects will always have water between them - unless their edges are perfectly dry. The same applies to Air, since it behaves similarly. Yet we do not notice the Air, just as fish do not notice the Water that surrounds them. So, does all Sense-Apprehension function in the same way, or are there different forms?

Taste-Apprehension and Touch-Apprehension seem to occur by contact, while the others function at a distance. But even hard and soft are apprehended through something else, just as Color, Sound, and Smell are. The difference lies in the nearness or farness of the Medium. Some Apprehensions seem immediate; others, remote. This is why we fail to recognize that Apprehension often occurs through a Medium.

As noted earlier, if we apprehended all Touchables through a membrane and did not sense the membrane, it would be no different from apprehending in Air or Water - we would think we are in direct contact. But there is a difference: with Sight or Hearing, the Medium itself acts upon us. With Touch, we are not acted upon by the Medium, but along with it - just as one may be struck through a shield. The shield does not act on its own, but the blow and the shield strike together. Thus, the flesh and the tongue relate to Touch-Apprehension the way Air or Water relate to Sight, Hearing, and Smell - as Mediators, not as Primary-Organs. If the true Sense-Apprehension Organ for Touch were directly touched - like when a white Object is pressed directly on the eye -

there would be no Apprehension. So, the true Organ must be internal. Just as in the other Apprehensions, when an Object is placed directly on the actual Organ, nothing is apprehended; but when it contacts the Medium, Apprehension occurs. Thus, the flesh is only a Medium between the Touchable and the True Organ.

The distinctions of body-type - hot and cold, dry and moist - are the same as those by which the Elements themselves are distinguished, and were discussed in the treatises on Elemental-Structure. The Organ for these distinctions is the Touching-Organ, and the Capacity in which the so-called Touch first exists is one that is Potentially these opposites. For Apprehension always involves an affection. What is Actual in the acting Object produces the same in the Receiving Subject, insofar as the latter is Potentially so. This is why we apprehend not what is moderately hot or cold, but what is at the extremes - for Sense-Apprehension is a kind of Mean between opposites. It judges by being in the middle, Potentially both, Actually neither. Just as Sight-Apprehension Grasp both white and black by being neither, so too the Touching-Organ must be Potentially both hot and cold, but Actually neither.

Finally, Touch-Apprehension, like the others, relates not only to the Touchable but also to the Un-Touchable - that which either differs too little, as in the Air, or too much, such that it harms the Apprehension

Organ, like what is violently extreme. Thus, we have now given an outline of each of the Sense-Apprehensions.

12: Second Analogy (Form without Matter)

In general, we must understand this about all Sense-Apprehension (αἴσθησις): it is the Capacity to receive the Form-of-the-Apprehended (τῶν αἰσθητῶν εἰδῶν) without receiving the Material-Stuff (ὕλη) along with it. Just as wax receives the Imprint of a signet ring without receiving the iron or gold, though it receives the Imprint as-of iron or gold and not as iron or gold itself - so too each Sense-Apprehension Capacity receives an Alteration from the Color-Apprehendable, the Sound-Apprehendable, or the Flavor-Apprehendable, yet it does not Become any of those things. Instead, it becomes like them, according to a specific Rational-Structure (λόγος).

The Primary Sense-Apprehension Organ (πρῶτον αἰσθητήριον) is that in which this Capacity exists. It is the same in Underlying-Subject, but differs in Being (τὸ εἶναι). For even though the Apprehendable may have Magnitude, to be Apprehended is not to be a Magnitude. Apprehension is not the grasp of Magnitude, but rather the Rational-Structure and Capacity corresponding to it. This also clarifies why Excesses of the Apprehendables (ὑπερβολαὶ τῶν αἰσθητῶν) destroy the Sense-Apprehension Organs. When the Motion (κίνησις) caused by the Apprehendable is too strong for the organ to receive, it destroys the Rational-Structure - and that Rational-Structure is precisely the Apprehension. The analogy is that of the Harmony or Pitch of strings, which is destroyed when struck too forcefully. This also explains why plants do not Apprehend, even though they possess the Life-Principle and undergo alterations such as heating and cooling. They lack the proper Mean-State (μεσότης), and they do not possess the Capacity to receive the Form-of-the-Apprehended without the accompanying Material-Stuff. Instead, they are affected together with their matter, never receiving the Form apart from it.

One might raise a puzzle: Can something be affected by a Smell (ὀσμή) if it is not Capable of Smelling? Or by Color, if it is not Capable of Seeing? The same puzzle arises for the other Sense-Apprehensions. But if the Smell-Apprehendable (ὀσφραντόν) is the Smell itself, and if that Smell acts upon the Smelling-Apprehension Organ, then it does so only on what has the Capacity for Smell-Apprehension. Therefore, anything not Capable of that Apprehension cannot be affected by it. The same applies across all the Sense-Apprehensions: those that are Not-Capable of Apprehending a certain kind of Apprehendable are not Affected by it in the relevant way. This becomes clearer when we consider that Light and Darkness, Sound and Smell, do not cause Alteration in the material of the Ensouled-Body itself. Their Motion passes through the Medium - such as Air - and can even split wood during a thunderclap. In contrast, Touchable-Objects and Flavor-Elements do indeed produce Alteration, even in lifeless things. For these too are Affected, and therefore must undergo some kind of Being-Acted-Upon. Yet not every Ensouled-Body is affected by Smell or Sound. And even when affected, such bodies may not retain the Affection. For instance, Air may seem to "smell" when Affected, but it does not preserve the Affection. What, then, distinguishes Being-Affected from Apprehending?

To Apprehend a Smell is to be conscious of it. But Air, though Affected, does not itself Apprehend. Rather, its Being-Affected enables it to function as a Medium - a carrier for the Form-of-the-Apprehended. As Medium, it possesses no Apprehension, but merely conveys the Apprehendable-Form to that which does.

Book III: Powers of Knowing

1. Unity and Distinction

That there is no additional Sense-Apprehension (αἴσθησις, aisthēsis) beyond the five - namely Sight (ὄψις), Hearing (ἀκοή), Smell (ὄσφρησις), Taste (γεῦσις), and Touch (ἀφή) - can be demonstrated by the following account. If every Apprehendable (αἰσθητόν, aisthēton) belongs to one of these Capacities, and if we in fact possess the whole range of Sense-Apprehension Capacities, then necessarily, were any such Capacity missing, the corresponding Sense-Apprehension Organ (αἰσθητήριον, aisthētērion) would also be absent in us. Now, all things Apprehended through contact - as Touchable - are Grasped (λαμβάνειν, lambanein) by Touch-Apprehension. Therefore, if any further Sense-Apprehension existed, it would either belong to a different kind of Ensouled-Body (ἔμψυχον, empsuchon), or correspond to a Capacity not possessed by any Ensouled-Body already observed.

As for those Apprehended through contact, they fall under Touch. But those Apprehended through a Medium - such as Air or water - operate differently. If a single Medium can transmit several kinds of Apprehendables (e.g., Air conveys both color and sound), then the Sense-

Apprehension Organ using that Medium must be capable of Grasping both, or there must be distinct Organs for each. If several Apprehendables share the same Elemental property - for example, color and sound are both conveyed through what is Transparent - then the Ensouled-Being which Apprehends one might also be able to Apprehend the others, if suitably constituted.

Among the Simple-Elements, only two seem to serve as bases for Sense-Apprehension Organs: Air and Water. The eye is watery in composition; the ear, aerial. Smell arises from one or both. Fire belongs either to none, or to all, since no Apprehension occurs without a certain Heat. Earth appears not to serve as a Medium in itself, unless as a Compound in Touch-Apprehension. Thus, all Sense-Apprehension Organs are formed from Air or Water, and these are already evident in the existing types of Ensouled-Bodies.

So, all Sense-Apprehensions are accounted for among animals that are not defective. For example, the mole possesses eyes, though veiled beneath skin. Unless some other kind of body exists, or some Apprehension not belonging to the known Elemental Bodies, there can be no additional form of Sense-Apprehension. Further, there is no separate Sense-Apprehension Organ for the so-called Common Apprehendables (τὰ κοινὰ αἰσθητά) - such as Motion, Rest, Shape, Magnitude, Number, and

Unity. These are Apprehended not directly, but incidentally, by the specific Sense-Apprehension Organs.

Motion is Apprehended through change in position; Magnitude, through Motion - since what Moves must have Extent; Shape, through bounded Magnitude; Rest, through the cessation of Motion; and Number, through perceived interruption in succession. But each individual Sense-Apprehension Organ Apprehends only its own Proper-Apprehendables - never these Common-Apprehendables by itself. Therefore, it is impossible that any specific Sense-Apprehension Organ exists for these Common Apprehendables. To say that Motion could be Apprehended by the Eye directly would be like saying that sweetness could be seen.

When we perceive two things as the same or different, we do so by Grasping them simultaneously within a Unified-Apprehension. If we fail to Grasp them together, we only Apprehend incidentally - like identifying "the son of Kleon" merely because he is white, not because we recognize his lineage. Yet we do not perceive the Common Apprehendables in this incidental way. If we lacked a Shared-Apprehension-Capacity for them, we would never perceive them as such. We would see only whiteness, not Kleon's son; we would sense only color or motion, not the structured reality.

Each individual Sense-Apprehension Capacity sometimes incidentally Apprehends another's Proper-

Apprehendables. This is not because one Organ has another's Capacity, but because there is one Unified-Apprehension (μία αἴσθησις, mia aisthēsis) active within the Ensouled-Being, coordinating the Apprehensions simultaneously. For example, bile is Apprehended as both yellow and bitter - not by two separate acts, but through a Unified Apprehension operating across multiple Capacities. This is why we might confuse the one for the other - seeing something yellow, we believe it bitter.

Why, then, do we not have a single undivided Sense-Apprehension Organ for everything? Because we would more easily be deceived. The distribution of Apprehensions across distinct Capacities helps guard against error. If Sight alone Apprehended whiteness and magnitude together, we might always assume things of the same color to be the same thing. But since properties like Shape, Size, and Color are Apprehended separately, we are less likely to mistake them. Thus, the fact that we Apprehend the Common Apprehendables across multiple Organs is itself a sign that each contributes something distinct - and that the whole act of Apprehension relies upon a Unified yet Differentiated Apprehension Structure.

2: The Unified-Apprehension Capacity

Since we are aware that we both See and Hear, we must either Apprehend that we are Seeing through the Sense-Apprehension of Sight itself, or by means of another Sense-Apprehension Capacity. But if this other Capacity is the same as that of Sight - and the Object is the same, namely, Color - then either the same Subject would possess two distinct Capacities, or one and the same Capacity would Apprehend itself. And further, if the Capacity that Apprehends Sight is distinct from Sight itself, then an infinite regress would follow - unless we affirm a Capacity that Apprehends itself. Thus, the inquiry must come to rest at a First-Apprehension.

A difficulty arises: if to Apprehend-by-Sight simply is to See, and if the Seen is either Color or what has Color, then if one were to See the very Capacity that Sees, one would also have to See Color in that Capacity. But then the Seeing-Capacity would itself have to be Colored - which is absurd. It is evident, then, that Apprehending-by-Sight is not a Single Actualized-Activity (μία ἐνέργεια).

For even when we are not actively Seeing, we make judgments concerning both Light and Darkness through the Sight-Capacity (δύναμις τῆς ὄψεως) - though not in the same way. There remains, even in rest, the enduring Presence of the Sense-Apprehension Capacity. Moreover, the Seeing-Capacity may be said to be Colored only in a metaphorical sense: not because it materially possesses Color, but because it is capable of receiving the Form-of-the-Color (εἶδος τοῦ χρώματος) apart from the Material-Stuff (ὕλη). That is why, even when the external Apprehendable departs, Images or Traces (φαντάσματα) remain. These are retained as likenesses - Forms without Matter. The Actualized-Activity (ἐνέργεια) of the Apprehendable and the Grasping Apprehension are one and the same in operation - though distinct in their Being (τὸ εἶναι).

For instance, the Actualized Sound and the Actualized Hearing are one operation: for something may possess the Capacity to Hear without actively Hearing, and likewise the Capacity to Sound without actually Sounding. But when that which can Hear is actually Hearing, and that which can Sound is actually Sounding, the two Actualized-Activities coincide. The single operation belongs both to the Hearer (as Hearing) and to the Sounding-Thing (as Sounding). Though the activity is shared, its orientation differs - one toward the recipient, the other toward the source. Now, if Motion, Production, and Being-Affected (πάσχειν) take place within the Subject that is Affected, then the Actualized-Activity of Sound and Hearing arises in that which is Potentially capable of Being-Affected. Thus, the Active Operation does not reside in the agent alone, but also in the Receiver - where the operation is completed. Therefore, the Sound-Producing thing need not itself be Affected. The Function of what Produces Sound is the Sound itself, or Sounding; and the Function of what is Capable of Hearing is Hearing. Each, then, has both Potentiality and Actuality - just as in the other Sense-Apprehensions.

This same account (λόγος) applies across the board: the Apprehension and its Apprehendable, like Production and Affection, exist not in the agent alone, but in the Subject that is Affected. In some cases, both sides of this relation receive names: Sounding and Hearing. In others, only one side is named: Sight gives its name to Seeing, but we have no term for the Actualized-Activity of the Color itself. Likewise, we name Taste, but not the Active Operation of the Flavor-Element. Since the Apprehendable and the Apprehending-Capacity share one Actualized-Activity - though not the same Being - it follows that when both are in Actuality, they must be preserved or destroyed together. But in Potentiality, this necessity does not hold. Some earlier Natural-Philosophers rightly declared that without Sight, there is no white or black; without Taste, no Flavor. They were correct in one respect - Actuality - but erred in not distinguishing it from Potentiality. Both Apprehension and Apprehendable must be spoken of in two ways.

If Harmony (ἁρμονία) is a kind of Sound, and both Resonance and Hearing are in some way the same and in some way not, then Hearing must likewise participate in this unity-in-distinction. Since Harmony is, in essence, a Rational Proportion (λόγος), Hearing too must be proportionally structured. Hence, Excess - of Sharpness or Heaviness - destroys the Hearing-Capacity, just as Excess in Flavor destroys Taste, or Extremes in Light destroy Sight. For Apprehension itself is a kind of Rational Proportion. It is pleasurable when the incoming Movement is pure and well-mixed - when the Sharp, Sweet, or Salty are proportioned rightly. The same holds for Touch-Apprehension: it is the Mildly Warm or Cold that is pleasing, not the Extremes. In general, Apprehension is destroyed by what falls short or exceeds the Proper Proportion.

Each Sense-Apprehension is directed toward a particular Apprehendable Quality, and Apprehends differences among kinds - white and black, sweet and bitter, and so on. But how do we Judge that white differs from sweet? This difference itself must be Apprehended - and by a Sense-Apprehension Capacity. But flesh cannot Judge itself; and separated Capacities cannot Judge separated Apprehendables as different. Judgment must occur in a Unity. Even if you Apprehend one thing and I another, we both know they differ - but for this to happen, the Judgment must occur in a unified Capacity. The same Sense-Apprehension Organ must be able to Think and to Apprehend this difference. Therefore, it cannot be that separated Capacities Judge separated Apprehendables. Nor can things Apprehended at different times be Judged as different at once. Judgment must be unified in time and activity. Yet no single undivided thing can be Moved in contrary ways simultaneously. If Sweetness Moves the soul one way and Bitterness another, how can the same Judging-Capacity (κριτικόν) be both one and yet divided?

Perhaps it is like a point: one and indivisible in number, yet divisible in Being. In this way, the Judging-Capacity can Grasp divided Apprehendables while remaining unified. When it uses two "points," it judges division; when it is one, it judges unity. Let this then be our Account of the Origin and Structure of the Ensouled-Body that possesses Sense-Apprehension.

3: Imagination

Since the Life-Principle is most often defined by two distinguishing Capacities - its ability to Move spatially and its ability to Engage in Form-Apprehension and discernment - it is worth noting that both Form-Apprehension and Thought resemble Apprehension in their structure. In both cases, the Life-Principle is involved in discerning something and in recognizing what-is. Earlier thinkers claimed that Thought and Apprehension are the same, just as Empedocles said, "As things are present, they are known by humans." Elsewhere he states that Thinking appears differently to each person depending on what is present to them. Homer likewise suggests, "Such is the mind of a man." All these thinkers treat the Act of Form-Apprehension as bodily, just like Apprehension - and they treat both as operating by Likeness, whereby the Like recognizes the Like, as we explained earlier in our Account of Origin-Principles.

Yet if they were correct, they ought also to have spoken of Deception - for Deception is more familiar to Ensouled-Bodies than the mere reception of Truth, and the Life-Principle dwells longer in this Capacity. We are thus left to say either, as some do, that all Appearances are True - or else that Deception occurs through contact with the Not-Similar. But this contradicts the Principle that Like recognizes Like. And in fact, both Deception and Knowledge arise from the same Capacity and pertain to contrary outcomes.

It is therefore evident that Apprehension and Understanding are not the same. Apprehension belongs to all Ensouled-Bodies, whereas Understanding belongs only to a few. Moreover, even within the Capacity for

Form-Apprehension - where both Correct and Incorrect Apprehensions occur - we must distinguish further: the Correct is called Wisdom, Knowledge, or True Opinion; the Incorrect includes their opposites. But this too is different from Apprehension - for Apprehension, when restricted to its own Proper Capacity, is always True, and is shared universally among animals. Thought, by contrast, includes the possibility of Not-True and does not belong to any creature that lacks Language or Structured-Narrative. Imagination is also distinct from both Apprehension and Thought. Though it cannot exist without Apprehension, and no Assumption or Representation can occur without it, we must clarify why Thought and Assumption are not the same.

Assumption, unlike Form-Apprehension, is under our control. We can Imagine an image whenever we Will - just as those who train in memory techniques do, crafting internal Representations. But Form-Apprehension is not subject to Will. We are compelled either to recognize the Truth or to fall into Not-True. Furthermore, when we Imagine something Fearful or Terrible, we are immediately Affected by Fear; likewise, if we Imagine something Brave or Uplifting, our Ensouled-Body reacts accordingly. In Imagination, we respond Emotionally, as if we were watching a painting of the Terrifying or the Courageous.

Even within Assumption, there are various kinds - such as Knowledge, Opinion, Wisdom, and their opposites. But the differences between these must be discussed elsewhere. Regarding Form-Apprehension: since it is distinct from Apprehension, and since Imagination seems to fall between them, and Assumption is something else again, we must now clarify what Imagination is, in order to understand the rest.

If Imagination (φαντασία, phantasia) is the Capacity through which a representation becomes Present - and not in metaphor - then it must be a single Capacity through which we Discern and either Affirm or deny. Capacities of this kind include Apprehension, Opinion, Knowledge, and Understanding. That Imagination is not the same as Apprehension is clear for the following reasons.

Apprehension is either a Capacity or an Operation - like Sight or Seeing. But Imagination appears to persist even when neither Capacity nor Active Seeing is Present - such as in dreams. Apprehension is always Present; Imagination is not. And if Imagination were identical with Apprehension's Operation, then all animals would possess Imagination. But this is not so - for example, ants, bees, and similar creatures do not appear to Imagine.

Moreover, True Apprehensions are always True; many Imaginations are Not-True. When we are clearly Engaged with the Apprehendable World, we say, "This is a man," not "This appears to be a man." It is only when our Apprehension is faint or confused that we rely on Appearances. Even those asleep report seeing visions. But no Capacity that is always Truthful - such as Knowledge or Understanding - can be equated with Imagination, since Imagination can be Not-True.

So, is Imagination (phantasia) a kind of Opinion (δόξα, doxa)? But every Opinion involves Conviction - and yet one may hold an Opinion without full Conviction. Moreover, no lower animals possess Conviction, though many seem to have Imagination. Every Opinion entails Conviction, and Conviction implies Persuasion, which presupposes Structured-Narrative - yet many animals have Imagination and no such Structured-Narrative.

So Imagination is not a kind of Opinion, nor derived from it, nor a composite of Opinion and Apprehension.

Furthermore, Opinion and Apprehension are both directed toward the same Apprehendables. For instance, it is the combination of the Opinion that something is white and the Apprehension of white that gives rise to the Imagined (φαντάσμα, phantasma) image - not the Opinion of good and the Apprehension of white. When something Appears (φαίνεται, phainetai), we form an Opinion in response to what we Apprehend - not incidentally.

Yet things may Appear Not-True even when one holds a True Opinion - e.g., the sun appears to be a foot wide, though we believe it to be larger than Earth. One must either say we abandon the Opinion (though we do not forget it), or else that we simultaneously hold both True and Not-True Opinions. The Not-True arises when the underlying Apprehendable shifts, and Mind (νοῦς, nous) does not remain aligned.

So then, Imagination is neither any of the previously discussed Capacities nor directly from them. But since every Motion (κίνησις, kinēsis) requires both a source and a recipient, and since Imagination is a kind of Motion, it must arise from Apprehension and extend toward the Apprehendable. It is caused by Apprehension in its fully Actualized-Activity and must resemble it.

Thus, the Motion we call Imagination cannot exist without Apprehension and cannot exist in Ensouled-Bodies lacking Apprehension. But in those that possess it, many Actions and Experiences occur through Imagination - some True, some Not-True. Apprehension, in its proper mode, is always True, or nearly so.

Error may come (1) from Accidental Apprehension - e.g., saying "this is white" truly, but misidentifying the Object; or (2) from the Common Apprehendables, such as Motion or Number. It is in these that deception most often occurs.

The Movement arising from Apprehending must differ from Apprehension itself. For Apprehension, when Present with its Object, is always True. But the Movement that persists may not be - especially when the Object is far or faint. If no other Apprehension Capacity exists in Ensouled-Bodies lacking Understanding, then this lingering Motion is what we call Imagination.

And since Sight (ὄψις, opsis) is the most refined Apprehension, and since phantasia (Imagination) comes from phaos (Light) - because no Seeing occurs without Light - and since Imagination preserves the Likeness (ὁμοίωμα, homoiōma) of the Apprehension after the Object is gone, many animals act on its basis. Some do so because they lack Understanding entirely, like brute animals; others act as though their Understanding were veiled, as in Suffering, Illness, or Sleep - even in human beings.

Let this, then, be our complete Account of what Imagination is and why it exists.

4: Mind and Time

We must now examine the Capacity of the Life-Principle by which it Apprehends, Discerns, and Understands - what we call Mind (voῦς, nous). Whether this Capacity is separable in Magnitude or only in Structured-Narrative (λόγος, logos), we must consider what distinguishes it and how the Activity of Form-Apprehension (voεῖν, noein) occurs.

If Form-Apprehension is analogous to Sense-Apprehension, then the Mind must in some way undergo affection from the Form-Apprehendable - or something analogous. In that case, the Mind must be Unaffected in its own Nature, yet receptive to the Actualizing-Structure (εἶδος, eidos) - and it must exist in Potentiality, the same as the Form-Apprehended, though not in Actualized-Unity prior to the act.

Thus, just as the Sense-Apprehension Organ relates to the Apprehendable, so too the Mind relates to the Form-Apprehendable.

Therefore, since the Mind is capable of Apprehending all things, it must itself be Unmixed, Pure, and Unaffected - as Anaxagoras claimed, "so that it might rule." But in our terms, it must be so in order to Recognize. For anything that is already Affected or mingled with another is obstructed in its Apprehension. The Mind, therefore, must not possess any Actualizing-Structure of its own. Its very Nature is Potentiality - the pure Capacity to Receive.

Hence, the so-called Mind of the Life-Principle - by which it Thinks and Supposes - is, before it thinks, in Actuality nothing of what it apprehends. This is why it is unreasonable to suppose that the Mind is mingled with the body. For what would it become if it were? Hot or cold? Would it have an Organ, like the Organs of Sense-Apprehension?

As it is, the Mind is nothing in Actuality of what it is in Potentiality - and this is why it is rightly said that the Life-Principle is the place of Forms (εἴδη, eidē) - not the whole Life-Principle, but only its Intellectual part, and not in Actuality but in Potentiality.

This difference becomes clear when we contrast the Sense-Apprehensive and Intellectual Capacities. When Sense-Apprehension Organs are overwhelmed, Apprehension ceases: loud sounds destroy Hearing, bright lights damage Sight, and strong odors disturb Smell.

But the Mind, when it apprehends the most Form-Apprehendable Objects, is not hindered. Instead, it becomes even more capable of apprehending lesser things. This is because Sense-Apprehension always requires the Natural-Life Body, while the Mind is separable from it.

When a Capacity is in fully Actualized-Unity - when it possesses what we call Knowledge-in-Actuality - then it can operate through itself. At this point, the Mind can also Understand itself. This is a higher form of Potentiality: like the one who knows having the Potential to Activate that Knowledge, rather than one who has yet to learn.

Just as there is a distinction between Size and the Sized, or Water and the Watery, so too this distinction occurs in many things - though not in all. In some cases, the what-it-is is indistinguishable from the Matter in which it inheres. For example, Flesh cannot exist apart from the Material it informs, nor can Curvature exist apart from the Curved.

So when we say the Apprehension-Capacity judges things like Hot and Cold, we sometimes attribute judgment to the Flesh. But judgment must occur through either a distinct Capacity or by a Structural-Relation within itself - just as a bent measuring-stick can only judge Straightness if it becomes straight.

Likewise, when the Mind Apprehends things like the Straight or the Curved - Form-Apprehendables involving Abstraction - it does so through comparison within a continuous unity.

And if the "what-it-was-to-be" (τὸ τί ἦν εἶναι, to ti ēn einai) is distinct from the "what-is," then it too must differ - either in Subject or Mode-of-Being. For instance, if Twoness is to exist, it must be distinct either in what it is said of or in how it is said to be. Just as things separable from Matter require distinct judgment, so too all matters pertaining to Mind require a distinct kind of Apprehension.

But then, one might ask: If the Mind is simple, unaffected, and shares nothing in common with anything else - as Anaxagoras said - how can it ever Understand, given that Understanding seems to require being Affected? For whenever something Acts and something else is Acted-Upon, there must be some commonality.

Now, the Mind is said to Act, and the Form-Apprehendable is what is Acted-Upon. If the Mind itself is Form-Apprehendable, then either it is so in the same way as other things, or it must be rendered intelligible by something else - just as other things become intelligible when mixed with the Intelligible Medium.

But we have already distinguished different kinds of Change and Reception. If the Mind is Potentiality for all Form-Apprehendables, then before it Understands, it is none of them in Actuality. It must relate to them as a blank tablet relates to writing - before anything is inscribed, it is Potentially all characters. This is the condition of Mind: Potentiality for all Form-

Apprehension, but none of them in Actuality until it begins to Understand.

Moreover, the Mind itself is Form-Apprehendable, just like the things it apprehends. In those things that do not involve Matter, the One-Who-Apprehends and the Apprehended are the same. In such cases, Theoretical-Knowledge (ἐπιστήμη, epistēmē) and the Knowable (γνωστόν, gnōston) are one.

Why, then, does the Mind not always Understand? This question must be faced.

In things involving Matter, each Form-Apprehendable exists only in Potentiality. These composites are Material-Formed - and their Forms are not separable in Actuality, only in Account. But what involves Matter cannot possess the Mind, because Mind, as the Potentiality for all Form-Apprehension, must be without Matter.

Still, though the Mind lacks Matter, it can receive the Form-Apprehendable from what is Material. This is because it does not receive the Matter itself, but only the Actualizing-Structure - just as Sense-Apprehension receives the Form of the Apprehendable without its

Matter. Thus, even when embedded in Matter, the Mind Grabs the Form-Alone.

Just as in all of Nature there is one being that serves as Matter, another as Actualizing-Structure, and a third as the Composite Product - so too must these be distinguished within the Life-Principle. Mind, accordingly, is spoken of in two ways:

One is Mind-in-Potentiality, which becomes all things by receiving the Form-Apprehendables.

The other is Mind-in-Actuality, which makes all things Intelligible.

We must now speak of this second kind - Productive Mind (νοῦς ποιητικός, nous poiētikos). It stands to the Potential Mind as Light stands to Color: Light makes the Potentially-Colorful into the Actually-Colorful. Likewise, the Productive Mind makes the Potentially-Intelligible into the Actually-Intelligible.

This Productive Mind is separable, unaffected, and unmixed - for it is, by Essence, Actuality. It is itself the Actualizing-Structure. To Understand in Actuality is not just passive Grabbing - it is a kind of Making.

While the Potential Mind may remain inactive and may fail to Understand, the Productive Mind always Understands. It is like Light: always shining, always making Visible what can be seen. It neither comes-to-be nor is destroyed. As is said, "This alone is immortal and everlasting."

But we do not Remember it - because it is Not-Affected, and only the Affected belongs to the Capacity of Memory (μνήμη, mnēmē).

5: Desire

Just as throughout Nature there appears to be a Double-Principle - on the one hand, something like Underlying-Matter (ὕλη, hylē) within each genus, which exists as the Potentiality of all things of that kind; and on the other, something like the Cause and Productive-Agent, which acts upon that Potentiality and brings it into Actualized-Unity - so too must we recognize this same distinction within the Life-Principle itself.

Accordingly, there is one kind of Mind by virtue of which the Life-Principle becomes all things - that is, receives their Form-Apprehendables - and another by virtue of which it makes all things - that is, brings those Form-Apprehendables into Actuality. The latter is a kind of

Possession (ἕξις, hexis), like Light: for just as Light makes Potentially-Colorful things into Actually-Colorful, so too this Productive Mind makes Potentially-Intelligible Forms into Actually-Form-Apprehended.

This Productive Mind is separate, Unaffected, and Unmixed in its Essence; it is Actuality (ἐνέργεια) in its very Being. For what produces is always more honorable than what is Affected, and what initiates is more noble than what merely receives. It exists always in Actuality - it does not Understand Sometimes and Not-Sometimes - and when separated, it is precisely what-it-is in Essence. It alone is immortal and everlasting.

We do not Remember it, because it is Not-Affected. But the Receptive Mind - being like Potentiality (δύναμις) - is perishable. And yet, without this Passive Capacity, there would be no Thinking at all.

Just as in the individual person, the Potentiality comes before the Actuality in time, so here too. But in Being and in Nature, the Actuality is prior to the Potentiality. In this way, the Productive Mind corresponds to Knowledge-in-Actuality, while the Receptive Mind corresponds to Knowledge-in-Potentiality.

6: Coordinated Cause

The Apprehension of Not-Divisible Objects takes place in those cases where Not-Truth is Not-Possible. But in domains where both Truth and Not-Truth are possible, there is already a composition of concepts - of Intelligible-Contents (νοήματα, noēmata) - as if each were already a Unity. Just as Empedocles once said, "Necks without heads sprouted," and then later these parts were joined by Harmonious-Bonding (φιλία, philia), so too here: things that are initially separate become Unified - such as the Incommensurable and the Diagonal. And if such things are Coming-to-Be or Going-to-Be, it is the Mind that combines them - and with them, introduces the concept of Time.

Not-Truth always arises through a kind of combination. For example, to say "the white is not white" is to combine the Negation ("not") with the content "white." It is also possible to speak by division - for example, to say "Cleon is white" or "Cleon was" or "Cleon will be" - and yet each remains True. The Mind is what produces this Unity in each case.

Now, since the Not-Divisible may be Apprehended in two ways - either as Potentially Not-Divisible or as Actually

Not-Divisible - it is not contradictory to say that the Mind Apprehends the Not-Divisible when it grasps the "this." For the Actually Not-Divisible exists in Not-Divided Time. Just as Time itself is Divisible-in-Capacity but Not-Divisible-in-Actuality with respect to Extent, so too with the Apprehendable: we cannot identify what exactly the Mind Apprehends in a given part of Time unless that Time-span has already been divided - which it is not, except Potentially.

When the Mind Apprehends each part separately, it divides Time accordingly - yet this division introduces Length-like measurement. But when the Apprehension is of both parts simultaneously, the Time is likewise Unified across both.

However, that which is Not-Divisible not by Quantity but by Form (εἶδος, eidos) is Apprehended by the Mind in Not-Divided Time, through a Not-Divided Actualized-Activity of the Life-Principle (ψυχή, psychē). This kind of Not-Divisibility arises By-Coincidence (κατὰ συμβεβηκός, kata sumbebēkos) - not because the Objects or the Time are absolutely Not-Divisible, but because the Apprehension is of that which is Not-Divisible. Even in these cases, there remains something Not-Divisible - though perhaps not entirely Separable - which causes both Time and Magnitude to be recognized as Unified-Wholes. This applies across all Continuous-Kinds, whether in Time or in Magnitude.

The Point, or Final-Limit of division, is like a Negation - and this kind of Not-Divisibility is a form of Lack (στέρησις, sterēsis). A similar Account holds for other cases. For example: how does the Mind Apprehend the Evil or the Dark? It does so, in some way, by means of the Capacity of the Opposite. That which Grasps must be, in Capacity, able to Receive what it Apprehends.

But if something has no Opposite, it Apprehends itself directly and in Actuality - for it is Separate. In every proposition, there is an Assertion (φάσις, phasis) - for instance, an Affirmation (κατάφασις, kataphasis) - and these are always either True or Not-True. But not every type of Mind is True in this way: only that which Apprehends the "What-It-Was-To-Be" (τὸ τί ἦν εἶναι, to ti ēn einai) of something in terms of its Essence. This kind is True, not by saying "something about something," but by Grasping the very Being (τὸ εἶναι, to einai) of the thing itself.

Just as Sight is True in relation to its Proper-Apprehendable, so too with all forms of Apprehension directed toward Beings apart from Underlying-Matter - even though, in practice, a person might fail to Apprehend the white, this does not invalidate the Truth of Sight itself.

7: Thinking and Desire

The Actualized-Unity of Knowledge (ἐπιστήμη, epistēmē) is identical with the state of the Object-Known. The Potentiality of Knowledge comes earlier only in Time, and even then only relatively - since all things that come into Being arise from what already exists in Actualized-Unity. It appears that the Apprehendable Object brings about Apprehension by virtue of the Apprehender being already capable - that is, possessing the Capacity for Grasping. Yet the Apprehending Subject is not passively altered or changed. For this reason, the kind of change involved here is not the ordinary form of Motion. The Motion in Apprehension is not an incomplete Potentiality progressing toward an end, but rather an already Actualized-Unity. It is distinct from the Motion of what is unfinished.

To Apprehend, then, is like making an Assertion, or simply Thinking. But when the Apprehendable presents itself as Pleasant or Painful - as Agreeable or Not-Agreeable - the Life-Principle either gives its Assent or expresses Aversion: it Pursues or Avoids. The acts of feeling Pleasure or Pain consist in the Actualized-Unity of the Apprehended Mean, in relation to what is Good or Bad, or to things of that kind. Therefore, both Pursuit and Aversion are themselves Actualized-Unities; and the Desiring and the Avoiding are not distinct either from each other or from the Apprehension-Capacity. Their Being differs, but not their Operation.

In the Discursive-Capacity (διάνοια, dianoia) of the Life-Principle, Images (φαντάσματα, phantasmata) function analogously to Apprehensions. When the Life-Principle Affirms or Not-Affirms that something is Good or Bad, it either Flees or Pursues accordingly. Therefore, the Life-Principle never Thinks without a Phantasm. Just as Air shapes the Pupil, which then produces another Form within, so too with Hearing. In the end, all is Unified - there is one Apprehendable Mean, even though its Capacities of Being may be many.

As for how Sweetness and Warmth differ, this has already been discussed. But it must also be stated here in a different way: there is something that functions as a Term or Boundary. These are Unified by Analogy, and also by the Numerical Relation each bears to its corresponding Pair. Just as one pair stands in relation to itself, so does the other. For example, what is the difficulty in saying how like things Discern Opposites, such as White and Black? Let us suppose A is White and B is Black. Then C and D will relate to each other as A and B do. If the pair C–D exist in one thing, then their structure resembles the pair A–B. The Unity is the same; the Being, not identical. The same reasoning applies if A is Sweetness and B is Whiteness.

The Mind Thinks the Forms (εἴδη, eidē) within the Images.

And the Pursuit or Avoidance of things is determined by the Thinking Subject in accordance with how those Forms are established within the Images. Even apart from external Apprehension, when the Life-Principle Moves within the realm of internal Images, it behaves as though Grasping. For example, when it sees Fire on a Beacon, it recognizes that an Enemy is nearby. Sometimes, using only internal Images or Objects of the Mind, it Considers and Deliberates about future actions in relation to present ones. When it declares that "something there" is Pleasant or Painful, it either Flees or Pursues "here" - and so Engages in Action.

Even apart from Action, Truth and Not-Truth belong to the same Kind as Good and Bad. But when expressed In-Abstraction, they are different - though still related. What is expressed In-Abstraction is understood accordingly. For example: the quality of being Snub-Nosed, as Snub-Nosed, is not thought of as separate; but if someone considers only the Concave Aspect, it is separable from Flesh. So too with Mathematical Objects: they are not Thought as separated from Matter, but are Thought when one reflects upon such kinds of things.

In general, the Mind is that which Thinks the things in Actualized-Unity. Whether it is possible to Think something that is Separated in Being without the Mind itself being Separated in Magnitude - this question must be considered afterward.

8: Final Apprehender

Let us now recall the preceding Account of the Life-Principle, and begin anew by stating: in a certain way, the Life-Principle is All-Things-That-Are (τὰ ὄντα, ta onta).

For Things-That-Are are either Apprehendable or Intelligible, and the Life-Principle contains all of them - either in Potentiality or in Actualized-Unity. Just as Knowledge is related to the Knowable, so too is

Apprehension related to the Apprehendable. We must now inquire how this relation is structured.

Both Knowledge and Apprehension are divisible according to the kinds of things with which they engage. Potential Knowledge is directed toward what is Potentially Knowable, and Actualized Knowledge toward what is already Actualized. The Apprehending and Knowing Capacities of the Life-Principle are, in Potentiality, the same thing - though one is oriented toward Apprehendable things, and the other toward Knowable things.

It is necessary, however, that what is Received by the Life-Principle is either the Things Themselves, or their Actualizing-Structures (εἴδη, eidē). But it is not the Things Themselves - for instance, the Stone is not literally inside the Life-Principle - but rather the Form-Structure of the Stone. In this way, the Life-Principle is analogous to a Hand: for the Hand is the Tool of Tools, and likewise, the Mind is the Form-Structure of Form-Structures, just as Apprehension is the Form-Structure of Apprehendables.

Now, since there is no separate thing apart from Magnitudes, as it appears, the Apprehendable Objects are not themselves Separable. Yet within the Form-

Structures of Apprehendables, the Intelligible is also present. These include both what is spoken of In-Abstraction, as well as the Conditions and Affections that belong to Perceptible things.

Therefore, a human being who does not Apprehend anything cannot Learn or Understand anything. And even when one is engaged in Contemplation, it is necessary that some Image (φαντασμα, phantasma) be present - for Images are like Apprehensions, except they do not include Matter.

Imagination (φαντασία, phantasia) is thus distinct from both Affirmation and Denial, since Truth and Not-Truth require the Combination of Objects of the Mind (νοήματα, noēmata). But what distinguishes the Primary Objects of the Mind from being mere Images? Or perhaps even other Objects of the Mind are not Images in themselves - yet none of them occur without Images.

9: Passive Mind

Since the Life-Principle is divided into two primary Capacities - the one associated with all Ensouled-Bodies, and the other concerned with Judgment - we must now examine not only the function of Discursive-Thought (διάνοια, dianoia) and Apprehension, but also the Capacity responsible for Motion according to place. We have already given an Account of Apprehension and of Mind. What remains is to consider the Origin of Motion: What Capacity of the Life-Principle is its cause? Is it distinct in Form or in Magnitude? Or is it the Life-Principle as a Whole? And if it is a Capacity, is it one of those already named, or some further one?

From the beginning, this inquiry is marked by difficulty: How many Capacities does the Life-Principle possess, and how should they be named? For in a certain way, they seem countless. Some divide the Life-Principle into Rational, Spirited, and Appetitive Capacities; others into the Rational and the Not-Rational. But if one differentiates based on the Functions that produce distinct operations, the divisions multiply - for example, the Nutritive-Capacity, which is shared by plants and by all Living Beings; or the Apprehending-Capacity, which does not fall easily into either the Rational or Not-Rational side.

Then too there is the Imaginative-Capacity (φαντασία, phantasia), which by its own Nature appears distinct from all the others, yet is sometimes assigned to either one. These difficulties multiply for those who insist that the Capacities of the Life-Principle are Separably-Existing. Further still, the Desiring-Capacity appears distinct both in operation and in definition from the others. And yet, to separate them entirely results in absurdity - for Volition belongs to the Rational, but Desire and Spirit dwell in the Not-Rational. If we say the Life-Principle has three Capacities, then each would require its own Desire, which is incoherent.

Let us return, then, to the original inquiry: What Moves the Ensouled-Body with respect to Local Motion? The processes of Growth and Decay, which are common to all Living Beings, would seem to belong to the Nutritive-Capacity. As for Respiration, Exhalation, Sleep, and Waking, these must be discussed elsewhere, for they too are complex. But concerning the Capacity that causes Local Motion in the Ensouled-Body, we must now seek the answer.

It is evident that this cause is not the Nutritive-Capacity - for all such Motion takes place for a purpose and in relation to Imagination or Desire. Nothing Moves unless it either Desires or Avoids - unless it is Moved by some external Force. Even if an animal is dragged, pushed, or possesses an Organ for Motion, we must still give an Account of what initiates that Motion. Similarly, it cannot be the Apprehending-Capacity alone - since many creatures possess Sense-Apprehension, yet remain fixed and unmoving throughout life.

If, then, Motion neither occurs without purpose nor bypasses the Necessary Capacities (except through Deficiency), and if Ensouled-Bodies possess the proper Organs for Motion, then we must ask again: What is the cause within the Life-Principle? It cannot be the Rational-Capacity, nor what we call Mind. For Theoretical-Mind does not concern itself with things to be Done, nor does it command the Pursuit or Avoidance of things. Yet all Motion must involve Pursuit or Flight.

Even when the Mind considers such things, it does not issue commands. One may contemplate something pleasant or fearful without acting upon it - though the heart may be stirred or some other part affected. Even when the Mind urges action - commanding Pursuit or Avoidance - Motion may not follow. For one does not always act in accord with the Mind, but with the Desiring-Capacity - as is evident in the Incontinent, who act against their own reasoning.

We see this clearly in the practice of medicine: possessing Medical Knowledge does not itself heal. There must be some ruling principle that Acts upon that Knowledge - and this principle is not the Knowledge itself. Still, even

Desire is not the ruling cause - for the Self-Controlled often do not act on their Desires, but instead follow the rule of Mind.

10: Active Mind

It appears that there are two Origin-Principles of Motion: Desire and Mind - if we include Imagination (phantasia) as a kind of Cognition. For many beings are Moved by Imagination in opposition to what Knowledge (epistēmē) would dictate. Among the Animal-Kind other than humans, there is no Discursive-Thought, only Imagination. Thus both Mind and Desire cause Motion with respect to Place. But not every kind of Mind - only the kind that reasons toward an End, the Deliberative-Capacity or Practical-Mind. This is distinct from Theoretical-Mind by virtue of its aim.

Every act of Desire also aims at some End. Wherever there is Desire, there is also the Beginning of Practical-Mind. And what is Last in Thinking is what becomes First in Doing. Therefore, both Deliberation and Desire seem rightly to be causes of Motion. For the Desired-Thing causes Motion, and Deliberative-Thought causes Motion precisely because it begins from what is Desired.

Even when Imagination causes Motion, it does not do so without the presence of Desire. Thus what truly causes

Motion is a Unity: the Desired-Thing. If both Mind and Desire are said to Move, then they must do so by way of something common to them. But Mind does not Move apart from Desire - for Volition (boulesis) is itself a kind of Desire. And when one acts in accord with Reasoning, it is in accord with Volition. Desire, however, can Move contrary to Mind, since Appetite (epithumia) is also a kind of Desire.

Mind, in every mode, is directed toward what is Truly-Good. But Desire and Imagination may incline toward the Not-Good as well. Therefore, what always causes Motion is the Desired-Thing - either what is Truly-Good or what Appears to be Good. Not every Good causes Motion - only the Practicable-Good, which belongs to the realm of things that Can-Be-Otherwise.

It is evident, then, that the Capacity in the Life-Principle that causes Motion is what is called Desire. Those who divide the Life-Principle according to Capacities, if they divide them as absolutely distinct, end up with many: the Nutritive-Capacity, the Apprehending-Capacity, the Thinking-Capacity, the Deliberative-Capacity, and the Desiring-Capacity. These differ from one another more than, for example, the Spirited and Appetitive Capacities.

Desires themselves can conflict. This occurs when Reason and Appetite are opposed. Such opposition arises in those Living Beings who Apprehend Time. For Reason, attending to the Future, may command one to resist; but Appetite, drawn toward what is Present, urges the Life-Principle toward immediate Pleasure. The Present seems Good, simply because it does not consider what lies ahead.

In Kind, the Moving-Principle may be one - the Desiring-Capacity as Desiring - but in Number, the causes of Motion are many. There are three components: (1) that which causes Motion, (2) that through which Motion is caused, and (3) that which is Moved. Among these, the cause itself is divided again into two: (a) that which is Not-Moved, and (b) that which both Moves and is Moved. The Not-Moved cause is the Practicable-Good. The cause that Moves and is Moved is the Desiring-Capacity - for that which is Moved either stretches toward something or is itself activated through such Stretching, and this is a kind of Desiring-Motion. What is Moved is the Ensouled-Body.

The Instrument through which Desire causes Motion is already Bodily. Therefore, it must be understood as a joint Function of Body and Life-Principle. In sum: the Ensouled-Bodily Instrument that causes Motion is a structure in which both Beginning and End converge - like the construction of Joints, where Convex and Concave come together. One part remains at Rest, while the other is in Motion. These may be distinct by Definition, but inseparable in Magnitude. Every Moving Thing must be thus. In every Circular Motion, some part must remain Fixed, and from that Fixed Point, all Motion begins.

Therefore, the Ensouled-Body is Desiring, and in this way it is Self-Moving. But Desire never arises without Imagination. And all Imagination is either Discursive or Perceptual. The latter kind - Perceptual Imagination - belongs to all the other Animals.

11: After Death

We must also consider the case of Incomplete Animals - those Living Beings that possess only Touch-Apprehension. What is the source of Motion in these? Is it possible for them to possess Imagination (phantasia)? Or not? And can they possess Desire? For it seems that Pleasure and Pain are present in such beings. And wherever there is Pleasure and Pain, there must also be Desire.

But how could Imagination exist in them? Perhaps in the same indefinite manner in which they are Moved. These Capacities may be present, but in an indefinite and vague mode. Perceptual-Imagination, as has been said, exists in all the other Animal-Kind. Deliberative-Imagination, however, exists only in those capable of Discursive-Thought (dianoia). For to consider "whether this or that should be done" is already the work of Deliberation - and Deliberation requires that one measure against a standard, always pursuing what appears Greater or Better.

Thus, a Unity of Deliberative-Judgment can be formed from many Imagined Forms. This may explain why such animals do not appear to possess Belief (doxa) in the Strict sense: they lack the kind of Belief that arises from Syllogistic-Thought, though they may possess another kind derived from Imagination. Therefore, the Desiring-Capacity does not itself possess the Deliberative-Capacity. Still, Desire can overpower and Move Deliberation; at other times, Deliberation overcomes and Moves Desire - like one Sphere striking another. When Incontinence arises, Desire Moves even the Desiring-Capacity itself.

By Nature, the higher Capacity is always more Authoritative and Initiates Motion. In this way, we now recognize that Motion can arise in three distinct modes. That which pertains to Knowledge remains Still; it does not itself Move. For Universal-Understanding consists of General-Judgment and Structured-Narrative, while Particular-Understanding pertains to Individual Cases. The one says, "This kind of person ought to perform this kind of act," while the other says, "This person now is such a kind," and "I am such a person." This latter kind of Belief already causes Motion - not the Universal kind.

Or perhaps both are involved - but the Universal remains more at Rest, while the Particular initiates Movement.

12: Third Analogy (Medium Transmits Motion)

The Life-Principle responsible for Nourishment must necessarily be present in all Living Beings that possess a Life-Principle - from Generation until Destruction. For anything that comes into being must also undergo Growth, Maturity, and Decay; and these are impossible without Nourishment. Therefore, the Nutritive-Capacity must be present in all beings that both grow and decay. However, Sense-Apprehension is not necessary for all such beings. Those whose Natural-Life Body is composed of a single Element Body-Type cannot possess Touch-Apprehension. And without Touch-Apprehension, it is impossible for any being to qualify as Living. Nor can any being be said to possess Life-Principle if it is not receptive to Form-Structures (eidē) apart from Underlying-Matter. A Living Being must necessarily have some kind of Sense-Apprehension - if Nature does nothing in vain. For everything that exists by Nature does so for the sake of something; otherwise, it would merely result by Coincidence (kata symbebēkos), and not according to Purpose.

If, then, any mobile body lacked Sense-Apprehension, it would perish before ever attaining the Natural End toward which it was formed. How could it Nourish itself? For Stationary Beings have their Nourishment provided in the place where they arise. But for Beings-in-Motion, it is impossible to possess a Life-Principle - and especially a Capacity for Discernment - while lacking Sense-Apprehension. And if the being is not Stationary and also Generated, then it cannot lack Apprehension. Nor can it be Ungenerated, for what purpose would it exist? Would it benefit the Life-Principle, or the Body? But it benefits neither: the Life-Principle would not gain greater Thought, and the Body would not be made more fully itself. Therefore, no body that is not Stationary can possess Life-Principle without also having Sense-Apprehension. But if Sense-Apprehension is present, the body must be either Simple or Mixed. Yet a Simple Body cannot possess Touch-Apprehension. And Touch-Apprehension is absolutely necessary.

This becomes evident as follows: since a Living Being is an Ensouled-Body, and all Body is Tangible, and Tangibility is that which is Apprehendable by Touch, it follows that the body of a Living Being must be Touchable in order for the being to be preserved. All other Sense-Apprehensions operate through something else - Smell, Sight, and Hearing are mediated. But without Touch-Apprehension, a being cannot avoid Harm or grasp what is Nourishing. And without these, it cannot Survive. For this reason, Taste is also a form of Touch-Apprehension, since it pertains directly to Nourishment, and Nourishment involves Contact with what is Tangible. Sound, Color, and Odor do not Nourish; they produce neither Growth nor Decay. Thus, Taste must be a kind of Touch-Apprehension, since it arises from direct contact with what is Tangible and Nourishing.

These Sense-Apprehensions, then, are necessary for the Ensouled-Body. It is evident that no Ensouled-Body can exist without Touch-Apprehension. The other Sense-Apprehensions, however, exist either for the sake of Well-Being or according to the Specific Kind of Animal-Kind - not merely by Chance, but with respect to particular Kinds. For example, for Beings-in-Motion, it is necessary that these Sense-Apprehensions be present. For such a being to survive, it must not only Apprehend by Touch what is near, but also Apprehend from a Distance. This occurs when something Apprehendable

Moves a Medium that lies between itself and the Apprehending Subject - so that the intervening medium is affected by the Apprehendable Object, and in turn, affects the Sense-Capacity. Just as something that causes Motion in Space Moves another up to a certain point, and the thing that pushes causes another to push in turn - so too here. The first Mover acts without being acted upon; the last is acted upon without acting; and the Intermediate both acts and is acted upon. There can be many such Intermediaries.

The same applies to Alteration, except that here the Alteration occurs without change in location. For instance, if someone dips a stick into Wax, Motion occurs up to the point of Contact: the wax is Moved, but a Stone is not; Water, however, is Moved a certain distance. Air, by contrast, is both Moved and capable of acting and being acted upon across great distances - so long as it remains present. This is why, in cases of Reflection, it is more accurate to say that Air is affected by Shape and Color, rather than that Sight-Apprehension itself is bent or redirected. Up to a certain point, the Air is affected by what it receives. On a Smooth Surface, the Impression is continuous - so that the Apprehending-Capacity is Moved in a unified way, just as if a Mark made in the wax were transmitted uninterrupted to its outermost edge.

13: Concluding Reflections

It is evident that the Ensouled-Body of a Living Being cannot be composed of a single Element Body-Type - such as Fire or Air alone. Without Touch-Apprehension, no other Sense-Apprehension is possible. Every Ensouled-Body must possess the Capacity for Touch-Apprehension, as has already been made clear. The other Sense-Apprehension Organs, situated externally from the Element Earth, may arise as Organs of Apprehension, but they function only through Intermediary Media - they Apprehend by means of something else. Touch-Apprehension, however, occurs through Direct Contact - which is why it bears that name.

Even the other Sense-Apprehension Capacities, though ultimately dependent upon Touch, do so only Indirectly. But Touch-Apprehension alone appears to function by itself. Therefore, the Ensouled-Body cannot be made solely of such Element Body-Types, nor can it be composed purely of Earth. The Touch-Apprehension Organ is always situated at a kind of Middle-Point among all the Tangible Qualities. The Sense-Apprehension Capacity must be receptive not only to Earthly Qualities, but also to Heat, Cold, and every other Tangible Form-Structure.

This is why we do not Apprehend anything by means of Bones, Hair, or similar parts - because they are composed of Earth and are Inapt for receiving Tangible Differentiation. Similarly, Plants lack all Apprehension because their composition is overly Earthlike. And since no other Sense-Apprehension can exist without Touch-Apprehension, the Organ that is responsible for Touch must not itself be composed of Earth or any other singular Element Body-Type. It is evident, then, that if a Living Being is deprived of this one Apprehension, it Perishes. It is not possible for a being to lack Touch-Apprehension and still Live, nor is it possible for an Ensouled-Body to possess any other Apprehension unless it first has this one.

For this reason, the other Apprehendables - such as Color, Sound, and Odor - do not destroy the Ensouled-Body by their excesses, but may damage the Sense-Apprehension Organs themselves, and even then only Accidentally. For example, a loud Sound may destroy Hearing when accompanied by a Blow, or certain Odors may impair the Olfactory Organ by their Tangible Side Effects. Likewise, a Flavor might also present a Tangible Excess, and thus cause Destruction.

But it is specifically the Excess of Tangible Qualities - such as extreme Heat, Cold, or Hardness - that destroys the Living Being itself. Every Sense-Apprehension Capacity is destroyed by an Excess within its own Apprehendable Range. Since the Tangible is what destroys Touch, and since Touch-Apprehension is the Necessary Apprehension for Living, it follows that without it, the Being cannot Live.

Therefore, Excess Tangibility does not merely destroy the Apprehension Organ - it destroys the Being Itself, precisely because this Apprehension is the one it must necessarily have. The other Sense-Apprehensions, as already explained, are present not for the sake of Being, but for the sake of Well-Being.

Sight exists because the Ensouled-Body lives in Air or Water - because it must See, and because it exists in a Transparent Medium.

Taste exists for the purpose of discerning Pleasure and Pain, to Apprehend the Nourishing, and to Desire or Move Toward it.

Hearing exists for the reception of Signals, and the Tongue exists for the generation of Signals to Others.

In all these cases, the Ensouled-Body is equipped with Capacities for surviving and flourishing - but only Touch-Apprehension is required for Life itself.